Email Marketing Success

*Nurturing Leads and Driving Conversions with
99+ Email Marketing Templates, Including
Cold Email Strategies*

JOHN LEWIS

DISCLAIMER

The contents of the book "**Email Marketing Success**," including, but not limited to, the text, graphics, images, and other content contained within, are the exclusive property of the author and are protected under international copyright laws.

TABLE OF CONTENTS

INTRODUCTION

E mail marketing for businesses is not a novel idea. In fact, when compared to other internet marketing channels like social media, mobile device apps, and even search engines, email marketing may appear old-fashioned.

A lot has happened in email marketing over the last few years, and the discipline is still in motion. Consumers' changing behaviors and expectations necessitate the development of new email marketing tactics. Personalization and segmentation techniques are converting company newsletters from anonymous bulk emails to customized mailings.

Today, most customers read their emails on mobile devices, and checking for emails has become the most common activity smartphone users perform. Because of the fight for attention in consumers' email inboxes, more companies are emphasizing the value of well-designed emails that are personalized and contain relevant content, ensuring that the emails are opened and read.

According to statistics, email marketing has a broad reach and is one of the top marketing methods for return on investment. Nowadays, almost everyone has an email address, and most consumers prefer to receive promotional communications via email.

Furthermore, with smartphones, emails are always in users' pockets and may be retrieved anytime. According to recent projections, the importance of email marketing will continue to rise in the next few years. Any online marketing approach your firm chooses should undoubtedly involve email marketing efforts.

More than just sending out the occasional newsletter is required for email marketing. Marketers must now set up and maintain subscriber lists, produce and design relevant emails, and send them out systematically. For your email marketing strategy to be effective and successful, you must continuously leverage the technical alternatives available to optimize the process using contemporary analytical tools.

Despite widespread email usage, many entrepreneurs have yet to execute an effective email marketing plan for their firm because they don't know how or haven't recognized how powerful it can be.

Email remains the Internet's primary communication platform and will only grow in importance. More than 3.7 billion people now have email access, and over 3 billion non-spam emails are sent and received every hour of every day. If your company isn't already using this powerful and enormous marketing channel, you're passing up an efficient opportunity to contact your target demographic.

Why Invest in Email Marketing

Email marketing, like any other marketing method accessible to connect your company with consumers, has advantages and disadvantages. Before you invest in an email marketing application, you should understand what you're getting into. Email marketing is one of the most cost-effective ways to promote your products and services, but it is not without flaws.

Let's begin with the advantages. Since customers have been more receptive to email marketing over the last decade, it has more advantages than problems. Consider the following benefits when deciding whether email marketing is good for you and your company.

Affordability

Suppose you or an existing team member can manage your email marketing programs and learn how to utilize your preferred email marketing tool. In that case, it's a very cost-effective approach to communicate with many people who have expressed an interest in your products or services.

Email marketing service providers often charge cheap monthly fees for their software. They may charge you based on the number of people on your list, the quantity of messages you send each month, or a combination of the two. Some companies, for example, have options that allow you to send messages to a limited list for free or for less than $10 per month. So keep in mind that the price typically begins low and rises as you add more subscribers to your list or send a bigger volume of communications.

Effectiveness

The Direct Marketing Association's "National Client Email Report 2015" states that for every dollar spent on email marketing, the average return is $38. Of course, that return is not guaranteed, but it is quite attainable if you test, adjust, and optimize your efforts. Furthermore, according to Forrester's "Social Relationship Strategies That Work" report, individuals are eager to receive email communications from organizations. According to Forrester, people are twice as likely to join a company's email list as they are to interact with it on Facebook. In other words, consumers prefer email marketing despite the buzz around Facebook marketing. Email marketing is vital to any marketing strategy, whether you're using it to improve website traffic or conversions and sales.

Measurability

Most email marketing systems provide you with a wealth of information about your subscribers and their behavior. You can, for example, instantly learn who accessed your email messages and clicked the links in your messages. Using this data, you may test various aspects of your email campaigns, such as subject lines, delivery time, and more. When you build up email automation sequences, you can even track where customers dropped out of your marketing funnel and develop new strategies to keep them in the funnel and move them through it to conversion.

You may even combine your email marketing platform with Google Analytics to better understand your subscribers' behaviors. The data you gather could be used to generate additional email campaigns and ad retargeting strategies.

Personalization and Customization

Email marketing software allows you to customize your email communications easily. You may customize the layout, colors, graphics, fonts, and other elements to fit your brand and appeal to your target demographic. Many software includes simple drag-and-drop design editors, allowing you to rapidly construct a highly professional email message. Furthermore, tools with advanced sequencing, segmentation, and automation functions allow you to personalize every aspect of your email communications for your intended audience.

Personalized email messages typically have higher open and click-through rates. You can experiment with personalizing the subject line of your email messages by adding the recipient's name or by personalizing the greeting within the message body (such as "Dear Bob"). Personalization does not always work flawlessly, but if you are satisfied that your list has precise recipient names, it can make a significant difference in the success of your efforts. It's an ideal element to put to the test.

Segmentation

To whom are you sending emails? Do you know where they are in your marketing funnel and what they want or need from you to keep them moving through it to conversion? An email marketing application with segmentation features allows you to segment by age, geographic location, birth date, anniversary date (of when they became your customer), average order value, date of last purchase, and more (depending on the information you've captured from your subscribers). You can segment your subscriber list and send targeted email messages to certain groups of people based on the parameters you provide. For example, you could create an email automation that delivers a coupon to previous clients on their birthdays. This is an excellent method for increasing loyalty.

Segmentation can boost open rates, click-through rates, and conversion rates. Some email marketing tools include complex segmentation features that allow you to segment based on behaviors. For example, you might set up a sequence that sends an email message to your customer list offering a special deal on a product on your website. Those who click on the link in the email to access the offer are directed to a special landing page on your website, where they may click the "buy" button and complete their transaction. People who make a purchase would be separated from those who do not make a buy. Buyers would get a follow-up email sequence with relevant products and services, while non-buyers would get warnings that the discount was about to expire. To maximize conversions, your segmentation and automation processes can get quite sophisticated.

5

Relationship and Trust Development

Building a brand that consumers recognize and trust is one of the most crucial components of running a successful business. Email marketing lets you demonstrate your authority on your subject matter, giving consumers confidence that you know what you're talking about. They will form opinions about your brand based on the email messages you send, and when the time comes to buy, they will go with your brand.

This is especially true for companies that provide items and services where purchasing decisions are more complex or seasonal. Email marketing is one of the most effective methods for nurturing leads until they are ready to act and make a purchase. They are more inclined to spread the word about your business as they become more familiar with it and rely on the information you send to solve their problems, save them time, or simply make their life a little easier. Email communications are easily shared, and a recipient only needs a second to click the forward button and forward your message to another contact. As a result, email marketing may be a fantastic source of word-of-mouth marketing and brand endorsement.

Time-Saving

You may save significant time daily if you set up your email marketing tool, develop some email automation sequences, and integrate your email marketing with your website, Google Analytics, and other marketing programs. Instead of manually sending thank-you notes, confirmations, offers, and so on, you can set everything up ahead of time, turn it on, and let it run on its own.

It is critical to test your automations regularly to ensure that nothing has gone wrong. Because no technology is flawless, it is always better to be cautious than sorry. Join your automation lists and see what happens. If something goes wrong, fix it right away. A poorly planned, worded, or structured email message may cause considerably more harm than benefit to your organization.

Email Marketing Tools and Terminology

Email marketing technologies have grown alongside email marketing throughout the years. We've transitioned from mass email marketing to highly targeted, time-sensitive, and event-triggered email marketing. Consumers learned they wanted to hear about promotions, offers, discounts, news, and more from firms via email as spam filters improved and many organizations ceased sending unsolicited emails. They are more than happy to join brands' email lists in order to obtain this essential information.

Naturally, competition in the market for email service providers has increased. Not only are more organizations providing email marketing SaaS tools available, but these companies are also providing extensive feature sets within their software programs. All the tools and terminology can be complicated, so before you continue reading, spend a few minutes learning the important topics. Without this information, you may waste time and money on tools you do not require.

Marketing Automation vs. ESP vs. CRM

To begin, you need to understand the distinctions between an email marketing service provider (ESP), marketing automation, and customer relationship management (CRM). These distinctions are critical since the functions provided by an ESP differ from those provided by a comprehensive marketing automation platform or a CRM.

ESP (Email Service Provider)

An email service provider (ESP) provides software that allows you to send email messages to lists of persons at precise times. You may be able to construct several lists, segment those lists into smaller groups of people, and even distribute newsletters and particular campaigns that you design automatically. Typically, the ESP gives simple design capabilities to help you generate messages that look professional. An ESP may even provide attractive opt-in forms that you can place on your website to collect email addresses from new subscribers. Some ESPs provide simple automation tools that allow you to program a sequence of messages to be delivered to persons on your list at specified times or after specific behaviors (for example, when a receiver clicks on a link in a message).

On your website, an opt-in box appears, inviting people to subscribe to receive your email updates. Visitors can enter their email addresses in a field on the form. You may be able to put other fields in the form, such as name and address, depending on the ESP you're using. When visitors use the opt-in form to subscribe, their email addresses should be automatically added to your list within your ESP account.

Consider ESP's software a tool for establishing customer relationships and closing sales. Popular ESPs include MailChimp, Constant Contact, iContact, AWeber, ActiveCampaign, ConvertKit, ClickFunnels, and Emma.

Automation of Marketing

Marketing automation firms have created software that allows you to do email marketing, among other things. You may track leads from acquisition to conversion by integrating your email marketing, content marketing, online advertising, and other marketing initiatives with marketing automation software. This program aims to streamline and automate operations to save time and money. Furthermore, centralizing marketing efforts in marketing automation software enhances tracking, allowing you to understand better which techniques perform best and swiftly and efficiently alter your marketing budget.

Marketing automation is all about nurturing leads and moving customers through the marketing funnel. The program includes powerful segmentation features to ensure that highly targeted audiences receive the most relevant messages at the right moment. The automation features are also highly extensive, so a business can conduct much of its marketing on auto-pilot once set up. HubSpot, Marketo, SharpSpring, and Pardot by Salesforce are examples of popular marketing automation software vendors.

Customer Relationship Management (CRM)

A CRM is a sales tool, not a marketing tool (though some overlap exists). CRM software allows you to track a person's full relationship with your company. You may instantly view a person's contact information, interactions with that person, dates and notes about phone conversations, notes about the person's requirements and preferences, purchase history, and more.

CRM software aims to increase interactions between your company and its customers so that they are more inclined to buy and tell others how pleased they are with their purchases from you. When your salespeople have all of this essential information at their fingertips, they can quickly track prospects and close more deals.

Salesforce, Zoho CRM, Insightly, PipelineDeals, Nimble, and NetSuite CRM are examples of popular CRM software.

Drip Email Marketing vs. Email Automation

Email automation and drip email marketing are two more terms that can be confusing because they are frequently used interchangeably. Both words refer to automatically sending email messages to people on your list. In other words, you establish a sequence of messages and assign certain timings or actions to trigger the delivery of the next message in the sequence. Here are a couple of such examples:

- When someone subscribes to your email list, your email marketing software is set up to send a thank-you message and enroll the subscriber in a campaign that sends a follow-up message three days later ("drips") with useful information and links to your social media profiles.
- You email all your customers using email marketing software, offering a special coupon code that expires in two weeks. Everyone on the list receives a separate reminder message the day before the coupon expires if they do not open the message.
- You send out your weekly email, which includes information about your new ebook and a link to download it. If someone clicks on the downloading link, they are automatically linked to a second campaign that distributes further relevant content and invites them to your future webinar on the same topic.

Depending on how the campaign sequences are configured in the email marketing software, each of these examples could have many messages. Email automation (as opposed to marketing automation) and drip marketing mean the same thing. You're automatically sending messages to people depending on their actions or timing.

PART I

EMAIL MARKETING BASICS

ADDING EMAIL TO YOUR MARKETING MIX

It is more complex than converting traditional communication forms to electronic formats or previous, more expensive media in favor of email delivery to incorporate email into your marketing mix. Increasing your company's email marketing potential entails two ongoing tasks:

- Analyzing the benefits and weaknesses of each instrument and media type in your marketing mix
- Creating messages that operate well across numerous types of media to reach your goals

It takes some trial and error to determine which tools and types of media are likely to work together to have a substantial, positive impact on your organization. At the same time, some tools have apparent benefits for any organization. Email is one such technique because it is inexpensive, and the returns on permission-based email campaigns are often excellent.

When compared to other kinds of marketing, email marketing has the highest return on investment (ROI) per dollar spent, according to the quarterly Direct Marketing Association economic impact research. Combining email with other tools and media can boost both ROI. The following sections discuss the advantages of mixing email with other tools and media and advice for employing various combinations.

Combining Email With Other Tools and Media

Combining numerous tools and forms of media to send your messages is a practical approach to marketing your business. Still, you'll probably find it more cost-effective to rely largely on a few communication channels where delivering your message results in the biggest return.

One of the finest methods to improve your overall return on marketing efforts is to use email for targeted follow-up. Here's an oversimplified example of how a targeted follow-up can be used:

- Your company employs traditional marketing channels to contact new prospects. For example, if you own a pizza restaurant, you can deploy an employee with a sign on a busy sidewalk to interact with potential customers.
- You gather contact and interest information from prospects who reply to your first contact. In exchange for a free slice of pizza, you ask prospective customers for their email addresses and the kind of coupons they'd like to receive via email.
- You send emails with customized messages based on the data you collect. If a potential consumer expresses an interest in chicken wings, you may send them coupons for chicken wings. You can even request that your consumer print the menu you have included in your email and pass your offer to a friend.

Branding Your Message Across All Platforms

In marketing, you're likely to use various tools, media, and messages over days, weeks, months, and years to express everything required to attract and maintain a sufficient number of clients. Maintaining similar or identical design elements and personalities in your messages over time — branding —

reinforces each message and makes each subsequent message more memorable to your audience.

When consumers can identify your brand and the content of each message feels familiar to them, they are more likely to respond positively to your email messages. Plan all of your marketing messages as if they were one unit to ensure that each message incorporates design aspects that your audience will recognize when many messages are sent.

Here are some branding suggestions to assist you in making all of your marketing messages appear and feel the same:

Make your logo visible and readable in all print and digital mediums by using color schemes that look good both online and in print. If you want to take advantage of words-only marketing alternatives like radio, podcasts, and text-only email delivery, ensure you can communicate your brand successfully with words.

Using Fundamental Marketing Principles in Your Email Messages

Convincing customers to spend money on your products or services usually entails communicating one of two basic messages:

Customers are unfamiliar with your products or services. Your task is to educate people who are likely to require your products or services so that they will purchase from you. Your products or services are well-known and readily available. Your task is to persuade customers that your company is the finest option among the competition.

It almost always takes numerous attempts to persuade people to respond to a memorable message. Effective marketing communications also require a certain level of strategy and tactical thought for your messaging to stand out from the crowd.

Applying basic marketing principles to your email messages ensures that your marketing communications are in sync with your target audience and overall goals. Although you can apply literally hundreds of marketing ideas to the email techniques and approaches in this book, start by structuring your message strategy around a few fundamental principles.

Marketing messaging strategy is a continuous cycle comprised of three key steps:

- Identify your message and the ideal audience for it.
- Deliver your message utilizing the appropriate media for your audience and message.
- Evaluate your outcomes and determine your next message based on your experience and more sophisticated marketing ideas.

Choosing the Text for Your Email Messages

Email is an excellent marketing tool, but you can't simply send an email message several times and expect it to result in sales. Make your email messages as brief as possible; most individuals scan emails rather than reading every word. Clear and succinct messages are by far the greatest choice for email content, but at the very least, your messages should have the following elements:

Your Value Proposition: A value proposition is a statement that tells customers why they should pay for your products or services. A good value proposition convinces customers that your products or services solve a problem or meet a need better than anybody else's. Here are some value proposition examples:

- "Do not confine Rover in a cage during the holidays." Our pet-sitting services take the anxiety out of your vacations and allow your pets to enjoy the holidays in the comfort of their own home."
- "Would you like it tomorrow?" Our free shipping is the quickest on the market."
- "Our home equity loans can help you pay off high-interest debt, and our service is more personal than the big banks."

Information To Back Up Your Value Proposition: Value propositions rarely motivate people to purchase quickly. Most of the time, additional information is required to convince purchasers to act on your value proposition. You can include this helpful information with your value proposition in a single email message, or you may want numerous support messages distributed over time. Here are some examples:

- Testimonials and statistics;
- Directions to your office, store, or website;
- Incentives to persuade someone to take action;
- Images and other design elements to support the text

Several Calls To Action: A call to action is a statement that asks someone to do something in a specified way. People prefer to discard emails after reading them if they aren't instructed on what to do next, so calling for action is critical. For example, just because your phone number appears at the bottom of an email does not guarantee that people will pick up the phone and dial it. You'll get better results if you ask your audience to call you for a specific reason and then give them your phone number.

However, an effective call to action does not always necessitate an immediate purchasing decision. Your prospective clients may have to undergo several procedures before receiving a store receipt. Calls to action could include the following:

- "Call now and ask for a free consultation."
- "Click this link to add this item to your shopping cart."
- "Click this link to download the informational video."
- "Save this message to your inbox today."
- "Print this e-card and bring it with you for a free cup of coffee."

Choosing the most effective phrasing for your emails usually includes testing and educated guesses based on how your customer perceives your company and its products or services.

Here are some questions to ask yourself to help you decide what to say in your email communications. Instead of merely mentioning your personal interests, think about what your clients find helpful about your firm as you answer each question:

- What distinguishes your products or services?
- How can the characteristics of what you sell assist your customers?
- What sets you apart from the competition?
- Why are your distinctions worth paying for?

In a paragraph, summarize your answers to the last four questions. Try to keep your text to two lines or ten words or less.

Choosing the Design of Your Email Messages

Images and colors, for example, are key design aspects in every email message since they can emphasize the words you employ or make them feel different to the reader. Not only does a text-only email fail to reinforce and strengthen the value offer, but it is also difficult to scan and read. Simple design details can greatly impact how an email message looks and feels.

Personalized Email Messages

When you're enthusiastic about your company, it's easy to see practically everyone as a prospective customer. You may have identified a vast audience that requires your products or services, yet many individuals will not buy from you for one reason or another.

Simultaneously, pockets of opportunity for communicating your messages that you haven't considered may exist. You may improve the effectiveness of your email campaigns by targeting prospects and customers who are most likely to make a purchase decision and removing those who are unlikely to buy.

Creating Email Content in Response to Consumer Engagement

Your email content should be consistent with how consumers interact with your medium so your audience can internalize and act on your message. Consider the following comparison between sending a message via email and sending a message via a billboard.

Consider putting up a billboard near a highway where people drive 65 miles per hour. Suppose your billboard message includes two paragraphs of text and an office phone number, cell phone number, fax number, email address, and detailed directions to your office. In that case, you are unlikely to get good results because no one driving by on the highway can internalize such a detailed message so quickly.

Furthermore, even if the billboard's arrangement makes it easy for cars to notice, some information on it is difficult for people to act on. Drivers, for example, are unlikely to send an email to an unfamiliar email address in the body of a billboard message because they are (ideally) not in front of their computers at the time.

People interact with emails in much the same manner that they interact with billboards because they quickly scan the content of an email to see whether anything is worth responding to or reading in greater detail.

People respond to emails very differently than billboards and other indirect media. People who see a billboard must use another type of media (such as a cell phone or a computer) to contact the associated business, whereas people can actively answer email messages by utilizing the media itself. People, for example, can easily respond to an email by clicking a link in the email's body.

- Downloading a file via an email link
- Email forwarding or sharing
- Responding to the email
- Clicking on a phone number in a text message
- Displaying an email on a mobile device
- Printing an email
- The email was saved to their inboxes.

Evaluating Your Messages

Continuously evaluating the impact of your email communications will help you fine-tune your strategy and make informed changes as you plan future messages. Message evaluation starts with defining quantifiable goals. It then continues as you track and measure your results to see if your goals have been met. Measurable objectives could include the following:

- Increasing the number of visits to a website by a specific percentage
- Increasing the number of orders or purchases by a specific percentage
- Receiving feedback and information about a particular issue
- Increasing event attendance by a specific number of people
- Changing one's mind or perceptions over a period of time
- Increasing the size of your contact database by a specific number of contacts

Using an Email Marketing Provider (EMP), you can easily track and measure the effectiveness of your messages. An EMP shows you who opens your email and who clicks on the links in your email. However, not all of your email evaluations must be based on clicks. For example, you could suggest that folks call you for further information. Then, you may evaluate your message based on how many phone calls you receive and what people say when they call.

Reaping the Benefits of Email

Email may appear to be a low-cost method of delivering marketing messages. It is generally less expensive because it allows you to send personalized, targeted, and interest-specific communications to many people. However, the benefit of email marketing does not end with the expense. Email marketing has advantages over other types of direct marketing for both your company and the consumers who request and receive your emails.

Requesting Quick Action

You won't have to wait long to determine if an email message succeeded. According to statistics, 80% of email is opened within the first 48 hours of delivery. It doesn't take long for your audience to take instant action after opening an email because consumers may take action on an email with a single click of the mouse.

- Immediate actions include the following:
- Reading and opening the email
- Clicking a link and then the Reply button
- Sending or sharing
- Printing an email
- Keeping the email

Obtaining Feedback

Email is a two-way communication medium; even commercial email may be used to solicit input and responses from your target audience. People may simply respond to emails, and many customers enjoy sharing their ideas when it is simple for them to do so. Email feedback falls into two categories:

Stated feedback happens when someone;

- Fills out an online form;
- Fills out an online survey;
- Sends a reply or posts a comment

Behavioral feedback occurs when you track

- Link clicks;
- Email open rates;
- Emails sent to friends

Increasing Awareness

When was the last time you mailed thousands of postcards, and your customers began queuing around copy machines to duplicate them so they could slap stamps on them and pass the message to their friends? Email applications provide a Forward button that allows users to easily send a copy of their email to one or more people in their address book. You can also take advantage of an

Email Marketing Provider (EMP) to include share links in your emails so recipients can share them on social media. EMPs track forward and share links so you can see who is forwarding and distributing your emails.

Staying Top-Of-Mind

People who aren't ready to buy right away are more likely to remember you and your company if you regularly provide them with good material. Suppose your content is useful enough for your prospects and customers to save. In that case, they may create tags with your company name and begin saving your emails in a dedicated folder outside the usual inbox for future reference. Your message is transmitted anew when they pull them out and reread them.

BECOMING A TRUSTED SENDER

Spam-blocking and filtering technology has advanced significantly in recent years, yet everyone who uses email still interacts with spam on some level. The key difference between today's spam and yesterday's spam is that customers increasingly apply the term to unpleasant communications, whether or not they are truly spam.

Consumers are always wary of emails unless they know and trust the sender, and they are more than inclined to report your emails as spam to their Internet service provider (ISP) if they are unwelcome or do not appear trustworthy.

Every email marketing campaign must adhere to several legal and professional guidelines that govern commercial email. Consumers also want marketing emails to originate from a reliable source and contain the appropriate quantity of relevant content. Here are three official criteria for deciding whether your commercial emails are spam:

- Legal standards, as outlined in the CAN-SPAM Act of 2003 and the 2008 revisions to the Act
- Professional standards, as outlined by consumer advocates and the email marketing industry
- Consumer preferences, as dictated by consumers themselves

Observing Spam Regulations

Spam is so annoying that Congress enacted the CAN-SPAM Act of 2003 to assist in the prosecution of spammers. The acronym is derived from the Act Controlling the Assault on Non-Solicited Pornography and Marketing of 2003. Aside from names, the legislation renders certain email marketing practices illegal and defines several standard practices.

If you're sending emails to people outside the United States, you should learn about the laws of the country to which you're communicating. While parallels exist between the U.S., several variations could get you in hot water under the CAN-SPAM Act. It is beyond the scope of this book to discuss the regulations of every country where email is used; therefore, you must do your homework.

Determining Which Emails Must Be Compliant

The CAN-SPAM Act of 2003, as amended in 2008, applies to commercial electronic mail messages, which are distinguished from transactional or relationship messages under the statute. In general, the CAN-SPAM Act distinguishes two types of email messages, as follows:

- **A commercial email** contains an advertisement, a promotion, or content from a company's website.
- **A transactional or relationship email** is anything other than a marketing email.

Although understanding that some email messages fall outside the definition of commercial email is critical, it is also critical to realize that all emails sent in the name of your business can be interpreted as commercial by the recipient. It is best to ensure that all business-related emails are legally compliant.

According to the 2008 CAN-SPAM modifications, emails sent to others by a receiver may be subject to all CAN-SPAM restrictions. Consult with your

Email Marketing Provider to ensure that your forwarded emails are CAN-SPAM compliant.

Legally Collecting Email Addresses

Certain email address gatherings are banned under the CAN-SPAM Act, and you must obtain permission from your email list subscribers before sending certain types of information. (Instead of permission, the CAN-SPAM Act uses the word affirmative consent.)

Because potentially illegal techniques of collecting email addresses aren't always obvious, the best practice is to ensure that you have specific authorization to send emails to everyone on your list. Following are some best practices for avoiding possibly permission-less email addresses:

- Never buy an email list from a provider that permits you to save the addresses in a data file. Email addresses stored in a data file can be easily purchased and sold, and email addresses sold in this manner are practically never gathered with specific consent for third-party use.
- Email addresses should never be obtained from websites or other internet directories. We advise against this practice because you do not have the owner's affirmative consent.
- Use an email address collection service at your own risk. You should not utilize such services unless you receive confirmed consent for third-party use from each subscriber.
- Don't use another company's email list or send emails to an email list. Those subscribers did not expressly want to receive your emails.
- Rent an email list only if you are confident that the list rental company practices are legal. Most rental firms do not have explicit third-party permission lists.

Including Required Content in Your Emails

The CAN-SPAM Act demands that specific content be included in your emails. To stay CAN-SPAM compliant, include the following in your emails:

- Allow your subscribers to opt out of receiving future emails. You must permanently remove anyone who unsubscribes from your email list within ten days of receiving the unsubscribe request, and you may not add that individual back without his specific agreement. When providing an opt-out mechanism, keep in mind that charging someone to opt-out or requesting information other than an email address and opt-out preferences is unlawful. Your opt-out process should also be completed by responding to a single email or visiting a web page. Your email marketing provider can supply you with an opt-out link that allows people to unsubscribe with a single click.

- Make sure your email has your actual address. If your company has many locations, as shown in Figure 3-4, specify your main address or the physical address linked with each email you send.

- Suppose you work from home and don't want to include your home address in every email. The 2008 CAN-SPAM modifications confirm that you can include your post office box address if the post office or box rental company associates the box with your real business address.

- Ensure your email header information accurately identifies your company and does not mislead your audience. Your From line, Subject line, and email address are all included in your email header. Ensure that the From line information in your email accurately and clearly represents your company.

- Check that your email's subject line is not deceptive. Use your subject line to deceive readers into opening your email or misrepresenting the offer.

- Check that your email explicitly says that it is a solicitation. The only exception is if you receive permission or affirmative consent from everyone on your list to send the solicitation.
- Check that your email complies with any applicable sexually oriented content rules. If your email contains such information, ensure the Subject line complies with the CAN-SPAM Act's additional rules and clearly conveys that the email's content is adult without being specific in how you characterize the content.

Improve Your Email Professionalism

Understanding and sticking to the ideas of the CAN-SPAM Act are crucial duties, but your emails will not impress many customers if they are barely CAN-SPAM compliant.

ISPs and EMPs anticipate that your email marketing initiatives will adhere to professional industry standards. Implementing your email marketing strategy under professional standards increases customer trust and distinguishes real e-mailers from spammers.

Using Complete Disclosure When Collecting Email Addresses

The CAN-SPAM Act advises you to obtain affirmative agreement from your email list subscribers before sending them a commercial email. However, the best practice is to include further transparency when asking for permission. Here are some ways to take affirmative consent to a higher level of professionalism:

- Ask for explicit permission to send emails anywhere you collect email addresses. Whether you hand out business cards to prospects in person or gather email addresses via a form on your website, be sure you get clear consent. It's also a good idea to preserve a record of your permission exchanges in case you get sued in the future.

- If you use email list check boxes on website forms, leave each one unchecked (unselected) by default. For example, if you gather email addresses through your website's shipping form, require your customers to tick a box to add themselves to any nontransactional email lists. Make sure the tick box also describes the types of emails your customer agrees to receive.

- Send a professional welcome note to all new email list subscribers. Ensure the welcome letter email arrives within 24 hours of the first subscription request and includes privacy information and a description of the types and frequency of emails the new subscriber will receive. When people join your email list via an online form, your Email Marketing Provider can send an automatic email.

- Send permission reminders regularly to ensure your email list members are still interested in your emails. You can send a business letter regularly or include a few phrases at the top of your emails asking your subscribers to confirm their interests.

Choosing When and How Frequently to Send

Consumers regard excessive email as spam; therefore, you must choose the frequency rate and timing of your emails. Frequency refers to the number of emails you send and the amount of time between each one. Common frequencies include

- Once
- Daily
- Weekly
- Biweekly
- Monthly

Balancing the frequency of each email communication with your audience's wants and expectations is more of an art than a science.

Consumers are happy to receive emails at nearly any frequency as long as the message's content stays relevant and helpful. Keep your content relevant to your customers, and they will most likely continue to enjoy your frequency.

For example, a stockbroker could get away with sending an email to his subscribers twice per day, provided the message only contained a single line of text indicating the current price of relevant stocks. However, the same stock broker would undoubtedly be in trouble if he used the same mailing frequency to send a promotional email inviting his customers to invest in various stocks because not everyone makes investment decisions at that frequency.

Although relevant content determines the appropriate frequency, you should be aware of the factors that most customers use to determine your emails' frequency. Consumers often rate your email frequency based on the following factors:

- The total number of email messages
- The size of each email
- How frequently do you ask them to act?
- The significance of the data you supply
- The moment

Choosing How Many Emails to Send

Determining the appropriate amount of emails to send is a delicate balance: sending too many email messages may overload your audience. If you send too few, you risk overwhelming your audience with too much substance in each one. The overall amount of email messages you send should correspond to your consumer's need for your information rather than your desire to give the information.

For example, a realtor may want to send dozens of emails to people actively looking for a home for weeks while sending only one email each month to those who rent an apartment and have no immediate plans to purchase a home.

Two factors usually determine the overall quantity of communications your audience expects:

- The number of times your audience goes through the buying cycle: If your prospects or customers buy your products or services once a week, sending 52 emails a year is a decent place to start. If your prospects or customers take months or even years to make a purchasing decision, you can base the number of emails you send on how often they will likely discuss their purchases with their peers. For example, if you sell once-in-a-lifetime holidays, you could establish an affinity club for previous vacationers and keep them talking about their experience by sending invitations to members-only social reunions four times a year.
- The amount of knowledge your audience requires to make a purchase decision: Some purchases are simple for customers to make, while others demand much more thought. If your audience requires a lot of information to explain a decision, increase the number of emails you send so you don't overload them with too much stuff in a few emails. Instead, send numerous emails, each with a small amount of material. Those requiring all of the information at once can be satisfied by providing a link to all your stuff on a website.

Estimating the number of emails required to distribute all of your information effectively can be as easy as dividing your information into equal halves or as complex as tracking interactions and delivering gradually greater volumes of content as your audience gets more engaged.

Although paying attention to your audience's demands is usually the best approach, your email content may influence the proper amount of messages to send. For example, the overall quantity of emails you send could be affected by;

- **The degree of variation in your content:** If your emails consistently contain the same basic message, you don't need to send as many as you would if your content was always fresh and new.
- **The theme of your content:** If the theme of your email incorporates frequency, you can match the number of emails you send to that theme. If your subscribers sign up for a daily weather update, for example, you must send 365 emails every year, whereas giving a quarterly financial report takes only 4 emails per year.

Choosing the Optimal Delivery Day and Time

If you send your emails when people are most likely to have time to read and respond to them, your audience is more likely to respond positively.

For example, suppose a substantial portion of your email list comprises people's work email addresses. In that case, you might want to avoid sending emails early on Monday mornings, when the individuals on your list are likely to walk into a crowded inbox and push your email to the bottom of their list.

When you do the following, you may decide the optimum days and times to send your emails:

- **Test for the best possible day.** Divide your list in half and send the same email separately to see which day gets the best response. If you have 1,000 email addresses, for example, you can send 200 each day of the week. Whichever day generates the best reaction can be your future mailing day.

- **Determine the optimum time of day**. After you've determined the optimal day, you may determine the best time of day. Divide your list and send the identical email to various people at different times on the same day.
- **For each list, create a master calendar**. If you send emails in multiple formats, use a spreadsheet or a calendar to organize them by frequency and format.

Planning enables you to visualize your email frequency and make modifications so that you don't send too many emails too close together and overload your audience. You can also use a calendar to help you decide when to send last-minute emails.

UNDERSTANDING THE MARKETING FUNNEL

If you own a business, you most likely already have funnels in place and are unaware of it. For instance, if you own a website, you have a funnel. This is because funnels aren't simply for marketing, though the vast majority do overlap in some way. The terms funnel, pipeline, cycle, and process are all used to describe various methods of moving consumers from awareness to action. By reading this book, you will discover how to construct the most efficient email campaign funnels and optimize your existing and new funnels to produce conversions and increase your return on investment. With that said, let us take a step back and define a funnel.

A marketing funnel is visually represented by a funnel similar to those used in cooking or automotive operations. It's a conical shape with a huge hole on top and a little hole on the bottom. You might use a funnel to pour oil or petrol into your car from a container. The goal is to get all of the oil or petrol down the funnel so that none spills out and into the car.

A marketing funnel, ideally, would do the same thing—ensure that each person completes a certain action. However, this is not a feasible option. The entire customer audience enters the funnel at the top, but unlike a funnel used for cooking or auto maintenance, not everyone makes it to the bottom. Filters and holes can be found along the route. You will lose folks, but your ultimate goal is to get as many of the right clients for the offer down the funnel as possible so they take action.

A marketing funnel is a theoretical and practical way to connect marketing strategies and tactics (including email marketing) to consumers' purchasing habits. To comprehend the marketing funnel, you must first comprehend the consumer purchasing process.

Let's look at it from a practical standpoint.

Assume you have an infinite marketing budget and wish to promote your new product in order to encourage people to buy it for the first time. You might purchase an advertisement to run during the Super Bowl. A large number of people will notice it, which means a large number of people will enter the top of your marketing funnel.

However, most of these consumers will likely not purchase your goods now or in the future. For a variety of reasons, they are simply not the appropriate match. You invest time and money in a marketing funnel to move people through it until they take action, but no one has the cash to invest in an audience of everyone. Your goal is to maximize the number of people who reach each level of the funnel without overpaying for people who are extremely unlikely to take the ultimate action you want them to take.

Marketers utilize various tools to drive individuals through the marketing funnel, including email messages, content, adverts, and more. A vast pool of potential customers is gradually (or fast, depending on the business, product, and audience) whittled down into smaller pools until a group of consumers emerges from the bottom of the funnel and completes the action (such as making a purchase).

The marketing funnel is organized into three sections: the top, middle, and bottom. Different forms of communication, content, adverts, and so on are employed at each point of the funnel to keep consumers moving through it.

TOFU (Top of the Funnel)

Everyone who isn't quite ready to buy is at the top of the funnel. At this time, they may not even realize they have a problem or a need. At the top of the funnel, your goal is to increase awareness of your product, service, or brand while attracting significant leads. You'd like to fill your funnel.

MOFU (Middle of the Funnel)

People in the middle of the funnel have already begun to look at different products, services, or brand options. They are gathering information to assist them in making a purchasing decision. They are narrowing down their options at this point of the funnel until they have picked a limited range of preferred items, services, or brands. You want to give them useful information so their interest in your offer grows even stronger.

BOFU (Bottom of the Funnel)

People at the bottom of the funnel are on the verge of acting. It's time to try to persuade your audience to act directly. This might be how you close the transaction or persuade someone to pick up the phone and call you. In other words, the individuals at the bottom of the funnel are eager to learn more about your product, service, or brand, so now is the time to advertise it. It is critical that you contact them often with prospects at this point. They've reached the tipping point, and it's up to you to figure out what kind of messaging, content, promotions, or other nurturing will give them that final push that will drive them to act.

Conversion Funnel Email Campaigns

Let's look at how to develop email marketing campaigns that successfully entice customers to perform a specific action (i.e., convert). The desired action could be to increase email subscribers, increase webinar sign-ups, produce free trials, close sales, or something else. You have an option. However, it is critical to note that email conversion funnels are typically composed of many components and pieces—not just a sequence of email messages.

Your email conversion funnel campaigns may contain complex automated email messages, landing pages, phone calls, appointments, free demonstrations, free trials, ebooks, checklists, webinars, depending on your industry, business, products, and services. You'll learn more about all of this throughout the book, but suffice it to say that good email marketing requires a lot of planning, setup, monitoring, and follow-up. It also necessitates extensive testing.

Fortunately, your efforts will be more successful if you can pinpoint where the consumers you're connecting with through email messages are in the purchase cycle and marketing funnel.

When consumers are not yet in the market, they are at the top of the funnel, and your email campaigns should focus on raising awareness. They've reached the middle of the funnel when they begin exploring choices, and your email messages should be focused on giving relevant, meaningful information to assist them in their investigation. Finally, when consumers reach the bottom of the funnel and are ready to purchase, you must ensure that your communications clearly express why your product, service, or brand is the best choice.

Generating Buyer Personas to Increase Funnel ROI

Before you begin developing marketing funnels, conduct customer research and develop buyer personas for your ideal customer as well as niche sectors of consumers so that you can produce better email marketing campaigns in the future.

A buyer persona is a textual depiction of a certain client group. Your goal is to uncover common motives and challenges so that you may develop marketing offers and communications that appeal to certain groups of people. Each buyer persona you design reflects a portion of your target customer based on data gathered via research in three areas:

- **Demographic Characteristics**. A person's physical and tangible qualities include age, income, gender, marital status, education, and whether or not they have children or own a home.
- **Psychographic Characteristic**. A person's emotional and intangible features include their beliefs and ideals. Human psychology has an impact on these traits.
- **Behavioral Characteristics**. A person's activities can be used to indicate consumer preferences, such as the sort of automobile they possess, their hobbies, the websites they visit, the magazines they buy, and the TV shows they watch.

You can interview your competitors' consumers, prospects, and customers to create buyer personas. Speak with your sales team, customer support personnel, and anybody else in your company who has a direct touch with your customers and may provide insight into their ideas, feelings, and behaviors. You can also conduct online, phone, or mail surveys with your present and prospective consumers.

Ask as many open-ended inquiries as you can when speaking with people to learn about their needs, issues, challenges, and motivations. The key to establishing great buyer personas is to engage in conversations. You can uncover common themes from these chats and use those themes to categorize clients into segments that will become your buyer personas.

Once you've gathered the necessary information, you may develop your buyer personas to serve as marketable consumer categories. Email marketing, copywriting, ad placements, content marketing, social media marketing, and other tactics will differ depending on the personas you're communicating with and where customers are in the purchase cycle and marketing funnel.

Communications for a teen girl's buyer persona would differ significantly from those for a male senior citizen's. Your buyer personas will be more sophisticated, but you get the idea. You must communicate with each buyer persona in their chosen language and modify your content and offers accordingly, or your results will suffer. You may accomplish this quite efficiently with segmented email marketing.

Avoid typical segmentation blunders when you create your buyer personas. Effective market segmentation, for example, is not a one-time event. To verify that your segmentation is valid, you must regularly analyze your segments and the general market. You must also be careful not to make overly broad portions, as they will not assist you. Similarly, too narrow segments can provide a negative return on investment simply because marketing to them is too expensive.

Also, avoid being a victim of information paralysis. Getting lost in the data may cause you to miss the most vital elements, or worse, it may prevent you from progressing. Finally, don't be deceived by size. Just because an audience segment has the most members does not guarantee it is the most profitable.

Getting It All Right for Email Marketing

Consider how your email marketing can be aligned with the marketing funnel and how buyer personas can help you make your messages more enticing to receivers. Rather than sending a message with a 15% discount to a large audience at the top of the funnel who may not be interested or who would have bought anyway without the discount, save that discount for messages sent to people at the bottom of the funnel who need that final push to buy.

Furthermore, instead of delivering a message with a basic instructional piece to those at the purchase decision stage of the consumer buying cycle, offer them demo videos and testimonials.

Similarly, rather than delivering a generic rival comparison table to consumers at the bottom of the funnel who are ready to make a purchase decision, provide tables tailored to each individual's buyer persona. It is quite likely that different characteristics and benefits would motivate different people. Your conversion rates will rise if that rival comparison table is personalized to each person's physical and emotional demands.

These are just a few ideas to consider while studying email advertising conversion funnels. Always keep in mind that there is a lot of planning behind any marketing funnel.

CHOOSING YOUR EMAIL MARKETING TOOLS

O nce you've invested time and money in establishing your own list of prospects and customers to increase your business through email marketing, you'll need to select the tools to gather those email addresses and send your messages. There are numerous email marketing solutions accessible today. Many offer extremely comparable features with little differences that may persuade you to choose one over another.

15 Favorite Email Marketing Tools

To get you started, here are 15 well-known email marketing services. It should be noted that this list excludes marketing automation and CRM solutions, both of which offer email marketing features. Instead, it exclusively provides email marketing-specific capabilities. CRM functionality may also be available as add-ons in some cases.

1. ActiveCampaign
2. AWeber
3. Campaign Monitor
4. Click Funnels
5. Constant Contact
6. ConvertKit

7. Drip
8. Emma
9. GetResponse
10. iContact
11. Infusionsoft
12. Mad Mimi
13. MailChimp
14. Ontraport
15. VerticalResponse

Remember that ESPs constantly change their tools, so do your homework before purchasing to verify you're getting the most up-to-date information and pricing. Your objectives heavily influence the technology you use for your email marketing expenditure. Do you simply want to collect email addresses and send everyone the same monthly newsletter? In the future, would you like to deliver communications based on the particular habits of your subscribers? Do you want to give out free ebooks or checklists in exchange for email addresses and automatically send them a link to that free content after they fill out a form on your website?

Your responses to these questions will influence your chosen email marketing tool. For example, if you merely want to send the same monthly newsletter to everyone on your list and have no ambitions to use more sophisticated email marketing strategies to build your business, MailChimp would most likely suffice. However, suppose you want to send highly targeted messages based on your subscribers' interactions with your messages, your website, and other factors. In that case, you'll need to use a different solution, such as ActiveCampaign or ConvertKit.

As a result, sit down and write down your short- and long-term email marketing goals. While moving from one ESP to another is possible, it is a time-consuming and rarely perfect process. You don't have to invest in the most advanced and expensive email marketing tool right now, but you should choose one that will fulfill your demands in the near future.

For example, you may want to send the same weekly message to your complete list now, but you may wish to divide your list into smaller groups with comparable qualities in the future. A health coach may want to send a different email to those who want to lose weight than those who want to control their diabetes. The coach may even launch new products or services tailored to each of those demographics and send promotional offers to persuade them to buy. Suppose the health coach's current email marketing solution does not provide appropriate segmentation options. In that case, the coach must switch to a new platform to pursue their marketing and business growth goals.

When selecting an email marketing provider, there are five main elements to consider: contact management, message design and setup, content and delivery, email management, and account administration and support. Let's delve into it.

Contact Management

When selecting an email marketing platform, look for one that allows you to easily gather subscribers' email addresses lawfully and identify who's who inside your subscriber list so that you always send the correct individuals the proper messages. Let's go over some of the characteristics to think about.

Opt-in Forms

How can you collect email addresses from people you don't know to add to your list?

You'll need an opt-in form (or many opt-in forms) where individuals may submit their email addresses. You could also request the names or other personal information of potential subscribers. Your email marketing tool should automatically add this information to your list, so you don't have to do anything manually.

Using an app that allows you to design visually appealing subscription forms is critical. A form that looks beautiful will increase your opt-in rate over a form that looks awful. As a result, use a tool that either provides professional-looking opt-in forms, allows you to customize the code for your opt-in forms so that you or a designer can make them look exactly how you want them to, or easily integrates with a separate application that provides high-quality opt-in forms, such as OptinMonster or Sumo.

Double and Single Opt-in Functionality

Subscribers that use single opt-in subscription forms just type their email addresses into your form, click a button, and they're done. Double opt-in forms necessitate some additional processes. After submitting the subscription form, the subscriber usually receives an email message. The message contains a link the recipient must click to confirm their subscription. They are not added to your email list if they do not click the link in the message.

To ensure optimum flexibility, you should look for an email marketing service that supports both double and single opt-in capability. You may wish to employ double opt-in to acquire new subscribers to ensure you have unambiguous authorization to send marketing communications to them. However, there may be occasions when requiring double opt-in is not desirable. It is essential to select an email platform that is flexible enough to match your continuing demands, and this flexibility should also extend to the opt-in criteria procedure.

Contact Management Methods

After you've gathered email addresses, consider how you'll keep track of those email addresses so you can deliver the correct messages to the right individuals at the right times. For this purpose, your email marketing solution should provide you with simple capabilities for managing your contacts.

You may manage subscribers in two ways with email marketing providers: list-based and subscriber-based.

List-Based Contact Management

If you use list-based contact management, everything in your email marketing account is based on contact lists. When a new contact is manually or automatically added via a form submission, that contact must be added to a certain list. Your emails are all dependent on the lists you make. Create a list of people who subscribed to your weekly newsletter, a list of people who sought product information from your website, a list of people who requested a copy of your free ebook, and so on.

The same contact may appear on many lists in a list-based system. It is your responsibility to remember what those lists were for and to ensure that you use all of the relevant lists every time you conduct an email campaign. When someone fills out an opt-in form, they are added to one or more lists, depending on how the form is configured in your email marketing service.

For example, someone may fill out a form to sign up for your weekly newsletter. As a result, that individual will be added to your Weekly Newsletter List. Later, they may fill out a form to get your new free ebook, and they will be added to your Free Ebook list.

If you want to send a promotional campaign in the future announcing a discount on a new product to all of your contacts, you'll need to send it to both of your lists to ensure you capture everyone. Unfortunately, this implies that some recipients may receive your message twice, and not all email marketing companies delete duplicates automatically when you send messages to different lists. That means persons on several lists may receive the same message numerous times.

Subscriber-Based Contact Management

Lists are the foundation of email marketing, but they have flaws. For example, SharpSpring, Marketo, and HubSpot use tags to maintain contacts rather than lists. Consider it this way. A list is similar to a massive file cabinet in which all your client's contact information is included without organization. You might purchase additional file cabinets to store the contact information of numerous consumers. However, if consumers are put into file cabinets with no structure, it might be extremely difficult to locate certain groups of customers when you need to contact them. This is where tags come in handy.

Tags are identifiers that you add to contact records to make it easier to find smaller segments of your email marketing list.

Tags function similarly to folders in a huge filing cabinet. Just like you may create folders in your enormous filing cabinet to group similar clients together, you can add tags to contact information in your marketing automation program to make it easier to discover them and give them the right marketing offers in the future. A customer may be filed in multiple folders in your filing cabinet based on specific characteristics or behaviors (e.g., everyone who purchased a specific product and visited your website's pricing page), corresponding to having multiple tags in your marketing automation software. When you need to find customers with a specific tag, you simply filter your contact list, and you're done. You can send email marketing messages to all of your contacts who have one or more tags of your choice.

Some email marketing service providers, such as ActiveCampaign, Infusionsoft, Ontraport, and ConvertKit, provide hybrid email marketing, marketing automation, and customer relationship management solutions, allowing you to manage your email marketing contacts with tags. These tags identify contact actions and behaviors, making sending targeted messages to specific audiences much easier. In other words, tags, a sophisticated marketing automation feature, are available in several hybrid email marketing platforms at a lower cost than typical marketing automation tools.

Rather than using multiple lists, you create a single list and choose who to send messages to based on the tags assigned to each contact. For example, you might have a master list of contacts, and based on how people interact with your subscription forms and email messages, tags can be applied automatically (or manually) to provide more information about each contact's preferences and activities. You can use tags to determine where a contact is in the marketing funnel, identify links clicked by the contact that indicate their interest in your products, or identify newsletters they've subscribed to.

Tags are extremely versatile and allow you to quickly and easily segment your contact list. However, it would be best to exercise extreme caution not to leave your tags out of hand. They won't help you if you don't know what they're for or why you made them.

Another disadvantage of using tags with only one contact list is the unsubscribe process. If a contact clicks the unsubscribe link in one of your email messages, they will be removed from your list and will not receive any further messages from you, regardless of your tags. This is because unsubscribes are based on lists rather than tags.

Many top marketers use a workaround of including a short message at the end of each email. For example, if a web design firm sends an email to its contacts about its new Facebook advertising services, it could include a line at the bottom of the message that says, "If you're not interested in Facebook advertising, click here and you'll be removed from these messages, but don't worry! You will continue to receive our other useful emails." It's not a perfect solution, but it's a popular choice if you want to power your email marketing with tags rather than lists.

Message and Design Setup

A bad-looking email message is unlikely to help your business. Because design reflects your brand and company, each email message you send should appropriately complement your brand promise. People are incredibly visual, and the design is the first thing they see when they open your emails. Select an email marketing solution that allows you to design professional-looking messages simply. Templates, customization, mobility, automation, and campaign setup are the four things to consider when comparing email marketing service providers.

Templates

Do you work as a web or graphic designer? If you don't, creating visually appealing email marketing communications can be difficult. Fortunately, email marketing providers address this issue by giving appealing templates from which to compose your messages. It is not necessary to be a designer to use them. Most of the time, these templates are simple to change with a drag-and-drop editing tool. Simply drag the sections around, add additional sections as needed, enter your text, and upload photographs, and you're done. Look for an email marketing service provider that includes a selection of templates with your membership rather than as separate add-ons that you must pay for.

It's vital to understand that there are two schools of thinking on email marketing message design. According to recent research, simple text communications that look like ordinary, personal email messages perform better than elaborately designed HTML email messages with many images and colors. ConvertKit, a popular email marketing tool, only allows users to write and send plain text messages. These figures can fluctuate from year to year and depending on the methodology of the studies, so consider testing both sorts of designs to discover which works best for your audience. Of course, to test both, your email marketing platform must support both.

Customization

Template customization is excellent, but sometimes, you need even more customization for your email marketing communications. In that situation, you'll need an email marketing tool that lets you alter all colors, move parts wherever you want, add images and video however you want, and modify the coding used to generate the designs for your messages down to the smallest detail. Not all email marketing systems provide you with access to the raw code affecting your messages' look. If you require extensive customization options now or in the future, do your homework and choose a solution that offers them.

Look for an email marketing solution that makes its application program interface (API) code available to experienced users so that your programmers may design and integrate exactly what you need when you need it. For example, suppose you want to automate a process but require your email marketing software to communicate with your internal project management software. In that case, your programmers will need access to your email marketing software's API to construct that particular integration. Keep in mind that most small firms do not require this, but if you are one of the enterprises that requires considerable customization, it may be crucial to you.

Mobility

Because more people open and read emails on mobile devices daily, it's critical that your email marketing messages display and work properly on smartphones and tablets. In other words, mobile compatibility should not be an afterthought. It should be prioritized. Keeping this in mind, select an email marketing supplier who prioritizes mobile.

Email templates that are automatically tailored for mobile devices are required. Templates should also be sized to be viewed on both desktop and mobile devices (600 pixels wide is ideal). Images should be kept in a way that allows them to load rapidly on all devices, and typefaces should be readable across various devices.

Campaigns and Automation

This is where email marketing truly shines. Different email service providers refer to individual email messages vs. sequences of email messages differently. In this book, the terms "automation" and "campaign" will be used interchangeably. Email automations are communications sent out sequentially based on individual activities, such as submitting a form or clicking a link.

Simple email responders, such as the thank-you message sent after someone fills out your subscription form, are examples of automations. Campaigns are delivered by hand and contain only one message (as no messages are sent automatically after the first).

For example, you might set up an automatic to send an email whenever someone wants your new free ebook. The link to download the ebook might be included in the initial communication. The second message may be set to go out two days later (i.e., "drip") with important recommendations, and the third message could go out three days later with a discount on a product relevant to the ebook topic. You would, on the other hand, send a campaign every time you send out your weekly email. There are no follow-up messages or other automations associated with these messages.

Look for an email marketing service that allows you to send one-time campaigns and automated message sequences. Many ESPs offer drag-and-drop tools for fast configuring automations, including what action initiates them, when messages should be sent, and even what messages users receive based on what they click inside prior messages or other actions. Automations can be fairly complicated, and as your email marketing campaign expands, you'll want to leverage these features. However, you must select a provider who provides them.

Content and Delivery

After you've evaluated design elements, consider which email marketing solutions allow you to develop content that fulfills your objectives and which have the highest deliverability rates. Although many email marketing platforms make sending messages to your contacts simple, those messages aren't always optimized to provide the greatest outcomes.

Personalization and Dynamic Content

Personalization entails more than just including a contact's name in the subject line and greeting in your message. Personalization has grown to mean offering highly individualized content based on each contact's behaviors and choices in recent years. This form of shifting content is referred to as dynamic content, adaptable content, or smart content. Simply put, the substance of your communications varies based on who is reading them.

A retailer's recommendation feature is an excellent example of adaptive content. Have you ever been browsing a retailer's website and noticed a slew of suggested things on your screen that you might be interested in? These suggestions change based on your actions, such as search phrases and other products you've looked at. The content is tailored to the visitor.

With dynamic content, you can show offers to the appropriate individuals at the right time. For example, if you send a holiday discount campaign to your subscribers, you can include dynamic information in your message that shows customers which things they might wish to buy with their discounts.

Using the earlier pet supply store example, you could show dog-related products to customers who have previously purchased similar items and cat-related products to people who have previously purchased cat-related items. Instead of attempting to please a huge, diverse audience, you can utilize smart rules within your email marketing platform to show the most relevant content to each individual.

Dynamic content and personalization are becoming more popular, so even if you don't think you'll use it anytime soon, you might want to start using it sooner than you think. With that in mind, make sure to include it in your overall comparison when selecting an email marketing platform.

Testing

Because testing is an important part of email marketing, you should select an email marketing provider that allows you to test as many aspects of your campaigns and automations as feasible. A/B split-testing functionality is built into many email marketing systems. You can divide your audience into segments and present various messages to each segment using A/B testing. You should ideally just test one variable at a time.

You could, for example, test your headline or the time of day when you send your message, but not both at the same time. The reason is straightforward.

Suppose you test numerous items simultaneously and notice a considerable improvement in performance in one version of your message over the other. In that case, you won't know which piece was responsible for the improvement. Email marketers, like scientists, test one variable at a time.

Experimentation and testing are continuous procedures that should always be carried out. Your performance will suffer if your email marketing platform does not allow you to conduct enough testing. Do your homework and ensure that the supplier you select enables split testing and makes it simple for you to run split tests on all of your campaigns and automations anytime you want.

Inbox Preview

Send email marketing messages without previously seeing how they will appear in recipients' inboxes. You can send test messages to yourself, but this requires several steps. If you have to send many tests, your email setup could take a long time. With the touch of a button, many email marketing tools have useful inbox preview features that allow you to see what your message will look like in recipients' inboxes.

Look for an email marketing solution that enables you to see how your message will look in all of the most common email providers' inboxes, such as Gmail, Outlook, and Yahoo! Look for a solution that allows you to preview your message on desktops, smartphones, tablets, and various mobile operating systems. No matter how much time and effort you put into writing a wonderful email message, it is all for naught if what arrives in recipients' inboxes looks ugly or is utterly unreadable.

Email Management

Some inbox email marketing platforms have so many functions that they are difficult to use. Others are so simple that they may not provide the strength you require. If you become overwhelmed while reviewing email marketing solutions, return to your goals and allow them to lead you. Don't overspend, but make sure you have enough capability to exploit email marketing properly. The following are some administration and management aspects to consider when comparing email marketing systems.

Mass Editing

How simple is it to change several contacts in the email marketing tool? Do you have to access each contact record individually to make changes, or are there procedures you may take to modify multiple contacts at once? Can you, for example, alter all 100 or dozens of records simultaneously if you want to add 100 contacts to a list or remove a tag from dozens of contacts?

Businesses change, markets evolve, and your email marketing goals and strategy must be adaptable enough to grow alongside your company. If your email marketing platform is incapable of keeping up or requires hours of manual involvement to stay up, it is insufficient. That is why it is critical to consider your organization's future and email marketing plan while selecting an email marketing platform.

Integrations

Email marketing becomes far more effective when combined with your website, social media marketing, content marketing, online advertising, and other digital marketing methods. Choose an email marketing service provider that works with the other tools you use to manage your marketing campaigns.

When tools integrate, you reduce the amount of human effort required to maintain all of your systems and programs in sync.

Your email marketing platform should, at the very least, interface with Zapier, a technology that integrates web applications to streamline and automate processes. Many web-based programs, as well as the majority of popular email marketing applications, interact with Zapier. You may also wish to combine your email marketing software with your invoicing, online calendar, e-commerce site, landing page, customer relationship management, online courses, customer service or online chat, help desk, and website analytics. The more connectors your email marketing service provider has, the more tasks you can automate to save time.

Customer Relationship Management (CRM)

Some email marketing systems, such as ActiveCampaign, ConvertKit, Infusionsoft, and Ontraport, also include various CRM capabilities. If CRM is crucial to you, but you are not ready to invest in or need a full-fledged CRM product like Salesforce or SharpSpring, one of these email marketing tools can be a good fit. A CRM-enabled email marketing technology allows you to easily follow contacts through your email marketing funnels, track their engagements with your communications, and close deals with them.

Some CRM-enabled email marketing technologies enable you to automate sales tasks and notifications, track sales activities, and qualify and score leads at various sales pipeline stages. It can become extremely complicated, allowing you to capture, nurture, and complete offers using bespoke sales processes and automations that you create. Choosing an email marketing solution with CRM functionality may make sense depending on your business, sales, and growth objectives.

Performance Tracking and Repor

How can you know if your email marketing efforts are effective if you can't track your outcomes? You don't, which is why your email marketing provider must provide you with access to simple reports and the option to obtain and edit raw performance data. Even if you aren't an analytics expert, you should be able to immediately discern which messages are being opened, which links are being clicked, and what needs to be improved.

Furthermore, select an email marketing platform that interacts with Google Analytics or your favorite website analytics engine, allowing you to trace contact behaviors from your email messages to your website and vice versa. These behaviors are critical for tracking success and developing campaigns and automations that deliver targeted, dynamic information.

Remember that testing is a critical component of email marketing success, and you'll need data and reports to evaluate which tests work and which don't.

Account Administration and Help

As with all software, things will go wrong while you operate your email marketing solution. It is critical that support is available whether you need assistance establishing your account, migrating from another email marketing tool, or executing any other job within the platform. Of course, you should be able to afford this support and all the other services you require.

Import/Export

When you start using a new email marketing solution, you'll most likely already have a list of clients to whom you'd like to send messages in the future. You might even have a list of subscribers already. If this is the case, you must be confident that you can quickly import those contacts into your new email marketing program. You should also be aware that they will be added to the proper lists or have the appropriate tags appended to their contact data once imported. This could be useful in the future if you collect an offline list of opt-in subscribers at a conference or event. You don't want to have to enter every contact manually.

At some point, you may need to export your contacts. For example, if you decide to change email marketing providers, you'll need to export your contacts in a format that can be imported into your new program. You never know what the future holds, so be sure you can export your contact list anytime. Don't worry: while the process for importing or exporting contacts may vary from one email marketing platform to the next, step-by-step instructions are often presented on screen.

Installation and Migration

When evaluating email marketing services, be sure to investigate how to set up your new account and migrate your data from another source. Some email marketing companies make the procedure simple and may even assist you in completing your move for free. Others will charge you a large amount to set up your account, followed by another fee to move your contacts and lists.

Remember that switching from one email marketing provider to another is never easy. You will need to make some changes to your campaigns, lists, and so on. It's unavoidable. However, you want to keep the quantity of data changes to a minimum, so seek a supplier that simplifies migrating. They should want your business, and it is in their best interest to assist you in effectively migrating so that you stay a satisfied, paying customer. Consider using a different email marketing supplier if the migration and setup processes are difficult.

Support

Depending on your technical ability, you may require continuing assistance or only on-demand assistance. At the very least, you should feel sure you can contact a knowledgeable person if something goes wrong or you can't figure out how to do something in your email marketing platform. Some email marketing service providers assist with an online knowledge base of text and video resources. Others provide phone, email, or live chat help. Some provide all or a subset of these assistance choices. Check that the ESP you choose provides the type of help you prefer.

Support hours and response times can also differ greatly. Some suppliers provide support 24 hours a day, seven days a week, while others only provide support Monday through Friday. The times when support is available may be quite essential to you, depending on your work hours. Furthermore, some email marketing providers give telephone help, but only as part of a more expensive plan or as an add-on option. Check to see what types of support are included with your chosen membership package.

Pricing can differ greatly between providers, so compare how each email marketing company charges users. Most email marketing providers charge a monthly subscription fee based on one of four pricing models: plan-based, subscriber-based, message-based, or freemium. The next section addresses each of these pricing models in greater detail.

Pricing Model Based on Plans

The plan-based pricing model determines monthly (or annual) rates for specific subscription plans. The cheapest plan has the fewest features, while the most expensive plan has the most. It makes no difference how many subscribers you have or how many emails you send. You are always charged the same amount regardless of your plan.

If you want to add more features, you must upgrade to a plan that includes those features. Alternatively, some email marketing companies offer some functions as add-ons, with separate costs for specific features, allowing you to pick and choose the capability you wish to add to your account.

Pricing Model Based on Subscribers

Subscriber-based pricing charges you based on the amount of contacts on your list. It makes no difference how many messages you send to your contacts. The amount of contacts saved in your account is all that matters. Typically, carriers offer a tiered price system that rises as customers increase. For example, if you have up to 500 connections, you could pay one fee, a higher fee if you have 501 to 2,000 contacts, a higher fee if you have 2,001 to 5,000 contacts, and an even greater fee if you have 5,001 or more contacts.

WARNING: If a contact appears on more than one list in your account, some email service providers that use the subscriber-based pricing model with list-based subscriber management capability count that contact multiple times. Remember this while you compare prices.

In addition to plan-based pricing, several email marketing providers use the subscriber-based pricing model. If you chose an email marketing company that charges users in this manner, you would choose a plan, and your fee would be determined by the monthly plan fee plus any premium charged based on the number of contacts in your account.

Pricing Model Based on Messages

Users are charged fees based on the number of messages they send per month under the message-based pricing model. It makes no difference how many contacts you have on your list. Instead, these companies count texts and charge you accordingly. If you have 100 contacts and send 10 messages to everyone monthly, you will be charged for 1,000 messages. If you have 1,000 contacts and send one message to each in a month, you will be charged the same amount—for 1,000 messages.

Like the subscriber-based pricing model, email marketing providers who utilize the message-based pricing model frequently set up tiers where the amount you're charged each month is determined by your tier. For example, the lowest tiered charge may apply to users who send 1 to 500 messages, while a higher rate may apply to customers who send 501 to 1,000 messages. Some email marketing companies combine the message-based pricing model with the plan-based pricing model, which is comparable to the subscriber-based pricing model.

Freemium

While it is unusual, some email marketing providers adopt a freemium pricing model in which the tier with the fewest capabilities or enables the fewest subscribers or sent messages per month is provided for free. You must pay to continue using the application when you reach the free tier's limits. You would then be charged based on the plan you select, the number of contacts in your account, the quantity of messages you send, or a mix of these pricing methods.

The freemium price model is popular for SaaS products because it allows customers to try an application and become so enamored with it that switching to another tool would be too cumbersome and time-consuming. It's incredibly effective for businesses, so use caution. It may be tempting to utilize a free tool, but it may not be the greatest option for you in the long run. As you discovered previously in this chapter, migrating from one email marketing provider to another is possible but rarely without complications. Choose the best tool for your needs, which may not be the cheapest (or free).

Make Your Final Choice

Reduce the list of email marketing tools that may suit you to three, then compare them using each of the parameters described in this chapter. Consider the long term, but don't overspend. You want a tool that allows you to be flexible and expand, but you don't want to be overwhelmed or spend money on capabilities you'll never use. Make a list and weigh the benefits and drawbacks of each tool. One of them will almost certainly win.

PART II

CRAFTING EFFECTIVE EMAIL MARKETING CAMPAIGNS

TYPES OF EMAIL MARKETING FUNNELS

I t is critical that you select an email marketing product that allows you to create automated sequences. These automations are produced when you build up processes to deliver messages to people on your list only once, leaving them to run independently without monitoring their performance. If you can't create automated message sequences, you can't create email marketing funnels that guide customers through your overall strategic marketing funnel. If you can't engage customers at every point of the marketing funnel, your email marketing outcomes will be limited.

Creating distinct email marketing funnels would be best to efficiently move consumers through your overarching strategic marketing funnel. These email marketing funnels are designed to draw new customers into your overall marketing funnel and prevent crucial prospects from dropping out over time. Depending on their goal, your email marketing funnels might be simple or complex, but they're always triggered by certain activities that identify a person as someone who could be pushed further into the broader marketing funnel if they received some extra push via an email message.

How to Choose an Email Marketing Funnel

You can construct hundreds and dozens of email marketing funnel campaigns to drive customers through your total marketing funnel. In fact, the only limitation is your imagination. On the other hand, all email marketing funnels fall into one of three categories: acquire, nurture, or convert.

Your objectives determine the type of email marketing funnel you construct. Is your list short? Do you need more leads at the top of your marketing funnel? If that's the case, you'll require an acquisition funnel. Do you need to keep leads engaged in the middle of the marketing funnel so they can progress to the bottom? Then, you'll require a nurturing funnel. Have you found clients at the bottom of the marketing funnel and only need a little shove to buy? The solution is a conversion funnel. As a result, you must determine where your audience is in the marketing funnel, your goals, and what type of email funnel you need to develop for each group.

Acquisition Email Marketing Funnels

Acquisition funnels have a single objective. They generate leads for your subscriber list, allowing you to market to them in the future. When developing an acquisition funnel, you must ensure that you are attracting the correct type of leads. Considering this, your acquisition strategies should appeal to your target demographic. They must be relevant, interesting, and beneficial to your target audience, or you will waste time and money generating a list of leads that will never convert into sales.

Conversion funnels should begin with a low-risk offer. Leads are frequently unfamiliar with your brand, products, or services. Based on their opinion of the value of their email addresses, you must provide them with something of equal or more value. Do not anticipate leads to make a purchase right away. That isn't what an acquisition funnel is about. Your goal is to collect as many relevant email addresses as possible to market to them and move them from the top of the funnel (where they are now) to the middle of the funnel and finally to the bottom of the funnel, where they will make a purchase and, hopefully, become loyal customers and brand advocates.

Consider this: if you approached someone you'd never met before at a professional networking event, would you start the discussion by saying, "Hi, do you want to buy my widgets?" You must first warm up your leads before attempting to sell to them. The same may be said for email marketing. Warm up your leads by providing them with helpful, entertaining, and relevant content and information before attempting to sell to them. Your list of leads will not expand much if you start with a hard sales pitch, but if you start with relevant information and create a relationship before going for the hard sell, your list will grow faster, and your conversions will be higher.

Tip: A quantity target is the goal of an acquisition email marketing funnel. You want as many appropriate customer prospect leads as possible in your whole marketing funnel. As a result, it's critical to understand some of the most frequent acquisition email marketing funnels that have been shown to increase subscriber lists successfully.

Lead Magnets

Lead magnets are pieces of free content that you distribute to your target audience in return for their email addresses. Create ebooks, reports, checklists, infographics, worksheets, or tutorials and use them as lead magnets to get prospects to give you their email addresses in exchange for a free download of the content. If someone is interested in your lead magnet, you might presume they are interested in your industry and the items or services you provide. That indicates they are likely to progress through the broader marketing funnel over time. This is why building relevant lead magnets is crucial to the effectiveness of your email marketing.

Live Webinars

Live webinars can be utilized to generate leads and nurture existing leads. Why are live webinars so beneficial? It's because attending a live webinar requires more commitment than downloading a free lead magnet. Subscribers sign up for a date to "attend," which puts you and your organization in their inbox and calendar. You might succeed with live webinars for lead acquisition if you can deliver important content in a webinar that people are likely to want, even if they've never heard of your business before. It's all about value; therefore, ensure your webinar outperforms the time commitment and perceived value of each lead's personal information and email address.

Nurturing Email Marketing Funnels

Nurturing funnels are used to maintain the proper people in your overall marketing funnel over time and actively lead them to the bottom, where they complete a purchase. Not everyone on your email marketing list is ready to buy when you sign them up. Depending on the sort of business, people's demands, and customers' locations on the buyer journey, moving them from prospect to conversion could take days, weeks, or months. That is why nurturing your leads via email marketing is critical.

Lead-nurturing email marketing funnels also assist you in keeping essential people from falling out of your funnel and removing leads who will never reach the bottom to make a transaction. You don't want to waste time or money promoting your company to prospects who will never become paying clients. Instead, you should invest your time and money in nurturing leads with whom you can form relationships so that when the time comes to make a purchase (which may frequently be accelerated with nurturing messaging), they select your firm.

Lead nurturing is about developing relationships with potential, current, and previous clients. Messages foster confidence between prospects and your brand. They may reduce impediments to individuals migrating to the bottom of your overall marketing funnel, and they maintain your brand top-of-mind over time.

Here are some popular nurturing funnels you can use to move customers down your marketing funnel.

Welcome

When someone subscribes to your list, send them a welcome nurturing communications funnel. The first message merely greets them. The second section contains connections to other information on your website or blog, and the third describes what you do and offer.

Trial Period

Provide a free trial on your website to give prospective leads a better understanding of your product's performance. Once someone signs up for the free trial, send a series of email messages to check in on how the trial is going, offer tips on how to use your product, provide sources for answers to questions, and finally, inform recipients that the free trial is coming to an end and how to make a purchase to continue using your product.

Anniversary Funnel

Send your anniversary nurturing funnel on the anniversary date when someone joined your list, made a special purchase, or completed another significant action. The first communication expresses gratitude for their earlier action. The second message reminds them of some of the benefits they receive from their relationship with you, and the third message includes links to products that have been chosen specifically for them based on their previous purchases and actions.

Survey

People enjoy giving their ideas, so they are more likely to reply to surveys sent to them if they are relevant and take little time to complete. Providing a survey to your subscribers is a terrific method to re-engage them, ensuring you're providing them with the most valuable content and letting them know their opinions matter to you.

Begin with a message informing them that the survey is coming and asking them to watch for it. Make it a point to clarify why you're doing the survey, what you'll do with the results, and how long it will take to finish. The survey should be included in your second message. You can use a free service like Google Forms to survey your existing list. If you require a more powerful survey tool, consider SurveyMonkey or QuestionPro.

Top-of-Mind

Sending useful content is an excellent approach to maintaining your brand in the minds of your followers. This is especially significant if your sales cycle is extended or you sell seasonal products. A top-of-mind funnel is a series of communications sent at specified periods of the year or when subscribers perform specific actions, such as visiting a page on your website or clicking a link in your email newsletter.

Each message contains a quick tip, a how-to article, or other piece of content that can assist them in resolving a problem relating to your product or service. The final message advertises goods or services.

Unsubscribe

What happens when someone unsubscribes from your mailing list? Do you let them go or try to maintain them by sending messages through an unsubscribe nurturing funnel? Before allowing anyone to unsubscribe from your list, try to keep them. Send them a note asking whether they're sure they want to unsubscribe. Give them reasons why they shouldn't; if your email marketing service provider permits it, allow them to unsubscribe from specific types of mailings.

For example, individuals may wish to unsubscribe from advertising messages while continuing to receive your email with instructional information.

Webinars

Webinars can be used to obtain leads (as previously stated), but they may also be used to transfer people from the top of the funnel to the middle and even from the middle to the bottom. For example, after collecting leads with a certain lead magnet, you could host a webinar that explains the next logical step consumers should take after reading, seeing, or using the lead magnet. This style of webinar pushes people to the center of the funnel. You could offer a discount on your connected service or product to shift them to the bottom of the funnel. The messaging in your webinar funnel will differ based on how you use it to move visitors through your overall marketing funnel.

Subscriber Retention

Some people on your subscriber list will eventually quit opening your emails. It makes little sense to keep sending emails to people who are uninterested in your products and services. As a result, it is critical to identify unengaged contacts and attempt to re-engage them. Create a subscriber re-engagement nurturing funnel in which you indicate that you haven't heard from subscribers in a long time and remind them of the fantastic content you've been sharing. Next, ask them if they still want to receive communications from you. If this is the case, they must click a link to remain subscribed. This is the most straightforward method for determining who wants to stay involved with your brand.

Conversion Email Marketing Funnels

Conversion email marketing funnels are designed to entice consumers to buy something or take another action straight away. The emphasis in this book is on employing conversion email marketing funnels to produce sales. Because these messages are sent to consumers at the bottom of the marketing funnel and ready to buy, conversion email marketing funnels are frequently used with other sales support duties, such as phone calls.

In conversion email marketing funnels, sending highly targeted, personalized messages is critical to your success. Ensure that the actions you want recipients to perform are relevant and specific. In other words, the call to action should be obvious. The remainder of this section introduces some popular conversion email marketing funnels.

Abandoned Cart

When a customer begins the checkout process on your website but does not complete their purchase, do not let them go. You should instantly implement an abandoned cart funnel that delivers a sequence of messages designed to entice customers to complete their transactions. The first message may simply say, "Did you forget to complete your purchase?" The second message could include a discount or free shipping, and the third message could play on the recipient's fear of missing out if they do not make the purchase."

Trial Upgrade

If you offer a free trial of your product to generate leads or get consumers to the center of your marketing funnel, but they don't buy it once the trial period is up, you should follow up with a trial upgrade conversion funnel. The communications in this sequence should remind them of the advantages they will lose if they do not update. Make sure you provide avenues for them to seek additional assistance. In this sequence, you can also send a message offering free setup, free training, or a reduction in the product price.

Free Demonstration

Free demos are frequently provided for sophisticated goods, particularly software-as-a-service (SaaS) products that consumers must see in operation to comprehend fully. People must not only provide their contact information and email addresses to receive a free trial, but they must also communicate with a salesperson. Because this is not a low-risk offer for individuals, free demos are typically used to shift leads from the middle to the bottom of the funnel or persuade people to make a purchase.

When someone signs up for a free demo, you must make them feel confident in their choice. Send a series of texts confirming the demo time and outlining the topics to be discussed. Before the demo, send a reminder message, and then send additional messages with valuable information, helpful links, testimonials, case studies, and other content that will remove any barriers to purchasing.

Add-Ons and Cross-Sell

When a customer is actively making a purchase on your website, this is the ideal opportunity to display complementary products to them. However, once the sale is complete, don't forget to offer complimentary products. Cross-sell and add-on conversion funnels can be created and distributed to customers after they purchase specific products or services. Your messages should introduce the products, explain why they are ideal supplements to the original purchase, and include customer feedback. You can even include a discount on the adjacent products to increase sales.

Promotions and Special Offers

Often, customers want to buy something but need a little push to do so. This is especially true given how busy people are these days. It's all too simple to put off making a purchase until it's no longer important or necessary. Create unique offer and promotion conversion funnels sent when users view specific pages on your website or on specified dates for seasonal or time-sensitive products to give consumers on your list that extra nudge. Send a message promoting the discount or promotion, followed by other messages telling customers when the offer expires and why they don't want to miss out on receiving the things they desire through the special offer. Including a countdown timer in these communications greatly enhances the response rate.

Refer a Friend

All of your subscribers are connected to other people both online and offline, which means that if you build refer-a-friend programs and promote them using email marketing funnels, your brand can spread far and wide. These funnels can be activated when someone on your list makes a purchase or whenever you want. Your messages should describe how the program works and what customers receive in exchange for introducing a friend. Check that they can share it both online and offline. Offer a unique discount to recipients who recommend friends to turn this into a conversion funnel.

Loyalty Programs

You can expand on nurturing subscribers that idea by developing loyalty programs that reward your most loyal consumers. Create a funnel that is prompted to begin based on the activities of a subscriber (for example, the subscriber purchases for the first, second, third, or whatever number of times you specify). Messages in this funnel should explain how the loyalty program works and make the customer feel unique for being a part of this select group.

Remember that devoted consumers can become your most outspoken brand supporters, so cultivate them with targeted, dynamic content. To turn this into a conversion funnel that leads to purchase right now, provide a discount when recipients join the program.

Remove Purchase Barriers

Getting rid of roadblocks to sales is an important component of maximizing the efficacy of conversion email funnels. These challenges differ substantially based on your sector and customer niche. Removing hurdles necessitates using an email marketing funnel with a sales call. Your email marketing funnel may include a case study describing how another client overcame a similar challenge. Follow-up letters should include more useful information and testimonials.

How to Build an Email Marketing Funnel

Building an email marketing funnel isn't tough, but it does involve some forethought, the correct tools, some technical knowledge (or access to someone who does), and some time. After deciding on an email marketing platform, review their tutorial videos or assistance pages to discover the precise steps the tool takes to build your funnel. Each tool is unique, and the processes change frequently as software is updated, so learn the correct steps from the source (your tool's help documentation or support team).

Assume you're creating a lead magnet email marketing funnel to gain new subscribers for your list. Create a form within your email marketing platform where people can submit their email addresses to download the lead magnet as the first step. You must also decide where folks who fill out this form will "live" in your email marketing contact database. That means you must create a list to include them when they submit the form. Furthermore, depending on whether your email marketing platform supports tagging, you may be able to add tags to characterize them further, which is vital if you employ subscriber-based contact management.

After you've generated your form and list, you can start building your email automation sequence. This includes defining the triggers that send the messages in your sequence and the content of each message. For instance, you could construct a sequence that sends a message containing the lead magnet download link as soon as the form is submitted. Next, you could program your sequence to send a follow-up message two days later. Following that, you may send another message a few days later, or you may decide to send one message to those who clicked the link in your message to download the lead magnet and another message to folks who did not click the link within 24 hours.

You can design your automatic series of messages as you want, but once completed, you must activate it (make it live and functional) and double-check that it is linked to the form you made to trigger it. Once you've confirmed everything is okay in your email marketing platform, put the form on your website or landing page so visitors can see and utilize it. To embed the form, you normally need to copy some code from your email marketing service and paste it into the code of your website. Many email marketing services have free plug-ins that integrate directly with WordPress and other website and landing page construction tools, making adding your form to your site simple.

After you've included the form, publish and test your website. If everything is in order, you may begin promoting it via social media, internet advertising, and so on. You must drive traffic to the page, or no one will know your lead magnet or fill out the form to join your mailing list. You can now develop several email marketing funnels to collect leads at the top of your marketing funnel, cultivate connections with leads in the middle, and convert those leads into sales at the bottom.

BUILDING AND GROWING YOUR EMAIL LIST

Email marketing is ineffective unless you have a list of people to whom you can send messages interested in your products or services. If you've collected email addresses from previous clients, you'll be well on your way. Every customer who has previously purchased from you has the potential to become a repeat customer. Email marketing helps to deepen their engagement with your company, allowing them to become loyal consumers over time.

Now that you've learned the fundamentals of funnels, tools, and how to ensure your messages are delivered, you can start increasing your list. Sustaining your brand's relationship with existing and previous consumers is crucial to your business's success, but you must also invest time and money in interacting with new prospects. Your business's growth will be limited until you consistently add more leads to the top of your entire marketing funnel. Cast a wide net, then utilize email, content, and sales approaches to move those prospects along the marketing funnel until they buy. According to Ascend2's 2017, marketers believe social media advertising, content marketing, and search engine optimization are the most successful ways to build your email list. Using these and other list-building strategies is critical to the success of your organization. Keep in mind that the power is on your list. You own it, and you may take advantage of it.

To expand your email list, follow these five steps:

- Create pertinent opt-in offers.
- Make efficient online opt-in forms.
- Drive targeted visits to your opt-in forms online.
- Show those visitors your offer.
- Increase the effectiveness of your online opt-in forms.

This chapter leads you through all five of these important processes, providing you with the foundation you need to build an email opt-in list of subscribers who want to hear from your brand and have the ability to move further down your marketing funnel with great email interaction and offers.

Create Applicable Opt-in Offers

The first step in expanding your email marketing list is creating an offer with a high enough perceived value that your target audience is prepared to exchange their email addresses for. Your offer could be a fantastic weekly email, a discount on a future purchase, a free trial or demonstration of your product, or a free tangible item known as an incentive or lead magnet by marketers. In other words, it's something that your target audience of prospects is so interested in that it pulls them like a magnet to your subscription form and motivates them to fill out the form to join your list.

These are the strategies you'll employ in the third part of the list-building process covered in this chapter. No matter how much you promote your offer online and offline if it isn't valuable enough to your target audience, no one will be interested enough to take action. This means that you will not only not receive traffic to your online opt-in form but will also not receive any subscribers.

Having said that, an opt-in form that does not guarantee a specific offer or free content as a lead magnet may just promote all of the fantastic information you'll share in your email newsletter. For instance, your opt-in form may simply state, "Sign up now so you don't miss out on the important news and tips you need to be successful."

You might make your offer more precise by writing, "Subscribe now and get a critical tip to grow your business delivered directly to your inbox every week." In step two, you'll learn more about creating opt-in form text. Still, these examples show that you don't have to give anything away other than the promise of helpful and important information to entice individuals to join your email marketing list.

Create Powerful Online Opt-in Forms

Most email marketing systems, such as ActiveCampaign, MailChimp, and Constant Contact, allow you to design opt-in forms easily. Simply construct the form as directed by your email marketing platform, copy the form code, and paste it into your website. It's a really straightforward procedure, but there's always a problem. Most opt-in form styles available in email marketing platforms are quite simple. The layout, colors, and even the amount or placement of copy may constrain you. Use a more powerful opt-in form tool to build your email marketing list.

Choosing an Opt-In Form Tool

You may use various programs to develop visually appealing opt-in forms that can be displayed in various places on your website. Most of these platforms provide libraries of free opt-in form templates that include graphics, fonts, and colors picked by professional designers. These templates are frequently tested and proven to convert visitors to subscribers so that you can use them confidently.

Many opt-in form technologies provide free trials or accounts with limited capability. Prices and features change frequently, so check each website to see what's new. Ensure that the product and package you select allow you to capture leads from your monthly traffic. Some restrict the number of visitors or form submissions permitted at various price tiers. Don't use your form if it appears wonderful but isn't visible to some of your visitors.

Furthermore, not all opt-in form platforms fully integrate with all email marketing tools. In other words, you can't log into your opt-in form tool, enter some information from your email marketing tool (typically a license key), click a button, and have your email marketing contact list automatically add or change contacts based on how they engage with your opt-in forms. That means you'll need to use another service, such as Zapier, to combine the two technologies, or you'll have to manually add or edit leads from your beautiful opt-in forms to your email marketing contact list. The goal of employing these technologies is to automate operations to streamline them. As a result, avoid using an opt-in form provider that does not interface with your email marketing platform.

Creating Opt-In Form Copy

Once you've chosen the tool to construct your opt-in forms, it's time to compose the form copy. The form copy must excite and compel your target audience to take action. They must comprehend the benefit of providing you with their email addresses and be comfortable doing so. To that end, here are seven goals you should strive for in your copy.

1. Respond to the question "What's in It for Me?"

"What's in it for me?" is an important question that any marketing message should answer for consumers. Copywriters use the abbreviation WIIFM to refer to this key question. Your message should clarify the benefits your viewers will receive if they fill out your opt-in form.

For example, if you don't provide a lead magnet and instead merely invite them to join your weekly newsletter list, what value do they gain from doing so? Rather than saying, "Subscribe to my newsletter," a fitness instructor could say, "Subscribe now and get my weekly exercise video to keep the weight off."

2. Explain the Offer

You must describe what customers will receive if they fill out your opt-in form or many of your website visitors may be hesitant to input their email addresses. Remember, people need to believe that what you give them is more valuable than their email addresses. Nobody likes an inbox full of spam or irrelevant communications.

People are quite defensive of their inboxes, so be very specific about what you're offering. In the fitness coach example above, the coach might have provided weekly workout recommendations, but the copy is very clear about what the coach offers subscribers—a weekly video with exercise tips.

3. Establish Expectations

Set clear expectations for what happens next when someone submits your opt-in form to enhance confidence. The first step is to tell them how frequently they will hear from you. Will you send them emails on a weekly or monthly basis? Will you send out promotional texts on occasion? Refer to the previous fitness coach example and note how the copy states subscribers would receive weekly communications. When leads submit the opt-in form, they know exactly what they'll get and when they'll get it. Suppose the fitness instructor intends to send promotional communications in addition to the weekly video messages. In that case, they may include a statement in the copy that states, "And occasional promotional messages announcing cool new products and offers."

4. Establish Trust

Many consumers who fill out your opt-in form will be unfamiliar with your brand or will just dimly recognize it. Because they may be unfamiliar with your reputation, it is critical to establish trust with them right away. They must think that you will deliver on the promises made in your opt-in form. To that end, include proof to support your assertions in your opt-in form.

For example, in your opt-in form copy, indicate how many other individuals have already subscribed, such as "Join 10,000 of your peers," "Join 10,000 people just like you," or "Join 10,000 like-minded people." If your target audience is a specific demographic, tailor your message to them.

For example, a fitness instructor with a top athlete customer could write: "Join 10,000 other high-performance athletes." This copy plays on people's fear of missing out (FOMO). Subconsciously, they'll believe that if so many other people like them are already on your email list, they should, too, or they'll lose out on essential information.

Furthermore, provide a copy of your opt-in form that assures customers that it is secure and that you will not divulge their email addresses.

Simple copy like "We promise we won't spam you or share your email address with anyone else" works great. This adds another layer of security that can influence how well your form turns visitors into subscribers.

Finally, if space allows, give one or more testimonials. If the testimonial is directly relevant to your opt-in offer, you don't even need to write any more text to accompany it. For example, if you're a fitness coach selling a free ebook and you have a testimonial from a subscriber who says they dropped ten pounds after following the advice in the ebook, include it on your opt-in form. No more copy is required because the testimony is so pertinent and particular. For less relevant or detailed testimonials, you may insert content before those that state, "Here's what other subscribers are saying about us." Of course, if a testimonial is too irrelevant and will not help convert visitors into subscribers via a specific form, it should be removed. Show less relevant testimonials on your website or another opt-in form where they will be more valuable.

5. Incorporate a Strong Call to Action

Your opt-in form should include a clear call to action, which is typically abbreviated as CTA. What action do you want folks to take after seeing your opt-in form? You're probably looking for people to enter their email addresses and click a button to get included in your email marketing list. As a result, make it very apparent how to complete that activity on your form. Use a large, visible call to action button in a color that contrasts with the rest of your form's color palette. After viewing your opt-in form, there should be no doubt about what a visitor should do next.

Your call to action copy should be particularly action-oriented. Include the copy on the button that leads people to your opt-in form. That is, the button on your form should not just state "submit." That is insufficient to maximize submissions. Instead, describe a specific action, use first-person pronouns (e.g., I, me, my, mine), and generate a sense of urgency whenever feasible in your button content.

For example, if you're simply providing a membership to your weekly newsletter, use language that says, "Sign me up now" or "I want my weekly tips." If you're giving out an ebook as a lead magnet, utilize a copy that says, "Send me my ebook now" or "Get my ebook now." Some opt-in form software even lets you insert countdown timers in your forms for limited-time offers. These are ideal for instilling a sense of urgency, especially if you're giving a lead magnet like a live webinar or a promotional contest with a set deadline.

6. Match the Opt-In Form Copy to the Design

Your opt-in form copy does not have to contain all of these items. Many opt-in forms are small, and there isn't much place for copy. Generally, the easier your opt-in forms are to use, the better. However, if you engage with a skilled copywriter, they can convey much of this information in very few words. It's an art form, and not every writer can master it.

Consider how much information you want from leads via your opt-in form. The more fields you add and the information you try to collect, the lower your conversion rates and the less room you'll have for compelling messages to attract and convert visitors into subscribers. Yes, having people's titles and company names is convenient, but is that information genuinely required for your future marketing efforts to function? Reduce the number of fields on your forms as much as feasible, and your results will improve.

7. Write Beyond the Opt-In Form

The opt-in form is not the end of your copywriting. What happens when that form is submitted? Will they be directed to a page on your website that expresses gratitude for their subscription? You should also write that. You should also email them, thanking them for subscribing and welcoming them to your community. If you promised a tangible incentive, such as an ebook or white paper, you must provide it by email.

Consider going beyond the opt-in welcome message. If you send a weekly email newsletter to all your list members, you can be sure they'll hear from you again soon after they read your welcome message. However, suppose you don't send a newsletter frequently (or at all). In that case, it's critical that you set up an email automation with a series of messages so you can maintain a relationship with each subscriber.

Drive Targeted Visitors to Your Online Opt-in Forms

Your target audience must view your opt-in forms for you to expand your email marketing list effectively. Having a list full of people who will never buy from you is useless. Fortunately, there are numerous measures you can take to direct the people you want to interact with to your website, where they will find your opt-in forms.

Here, we'll look at three ways to drive more qualified traffic to your opt-in forms. Remember that this list is not exhaustive but provides a good starting point for constructing your email marketing list.

Lead Magnets

Lead magnets are incentives to entice users to fill out your opt-in form. They may be ebooks, white papers, checklists, workbooks, templates, tools, or any other important content to help your target audience solve an issue or learn vital information. They could also offer promotional offerings like discounts or free trials. A lead magnet can be offered as a standalone reward via advertising, social media marketing, and other marketing strategies.

Third-Party Content

Third-party content is published on other websites to bring visitors back to your opt-in form. Guest blog articles are one of the most effective sorts of third-party content. Many prominent blogs allow you to submit free guest posts.

Each piece of content you publish on another website adds a new access point to your site. Include a link back to the page with your opt-in form, either within your post or in your author biography, which is published alongside your post. The idea is to discover sites where your target audience already spends time so that your guest articles send quality leads to your opt-in form.

The same can be said about various sorts of third-party content. Don't be scared to think outside the box when driving traffic to your opt-in forms. For example, seek people who ask questions about your lead magnet or your products and services in online forums, Facebook Groups, and LinkedIn Groups where your target audience will likely spend time. Participate in the discussion by including a link to your opt-in form for more information. You may do the same on popular question-and-answer websites such as Quora.com. However, do not market yourself in your comments. Instead, answer the question thoroughly and include a link to your opt-in form as a means for individuals to learn more.

Social Media

Social media marketing is a great technique for people to visit your website and fill out your opt-in forms. Share relevant content on your social media sites and links to your opt-in forms. Lead magnets are an excellent way to increase your list while employing social media marketing strategies. To increase interest in your lead magnet and drive visitors to click the link and submit your opt-in form, you can post sneak peeks from the lead magnet, photos, charts, related videos, and more. If feasible, pin any social media posts that link to your opt-in form to the top of your newsfeed.

You may do this on Facebook, Twitter, Pinterest, and other major social media platforms to ensure that people see your opt-in post before they view your other postings.

Social media can also be used to promote unique lead magnets, such as social media contests and giveaways. Set up a contest on Facebook, Instagram, Twitter, and other social media platforms using tools like ShortStack,

Woobox, or Wishpond. To make this work for list-building purposes, participants should be forced to enter the contest using their email address. Simply ensure that the prize has the same or less perceived value as an email address, or no one will enter the contest.

Advertising

Online advertising on targeted websites or through Google AdWords, Facebook ads, Twitter advertisements, LinkedIn ads, and other digital advertising services may be incredibly effective at increasing opt-in form submissions, especially if you're giving a lead magnet your target audience truly desires. Of course, quality copywriting is important, but without a strong lead magnet to promote, your conversions will most likely be lesser than they may be.

The key to success is to target your adverts to certain audiences. Many email marketers from various sectors have successfully developed their lists by advertising lead magnets through Facebook-boosted posts. The targeting tools are superb, allowing you to zero in on extremely particular individuals. Use an engaging image and great wording, and you should see an increase in opt-ins.

In addition to standard digital advertising, try native advertising (also known as sponsored posts or paid posts), which involves paying a website or blog to write a post on your behalf with a link back to your opt-in form page. Just make sure the website or blog states that the post was paid for, or you may be in violation of the Federal Code of Regulations' provisions on revealing content connections in online content.

Another effective method for converting visitors to subscribers is retargeting. Retargeting ads are presented to those who have previously visited specific pages on your website or demonstrated specific behaviors while engaging with your content. If you set up retargeting with a program like Google AdWords, people who leave your site will see your ad on other sites. Use a platform like Facebook advertising to set up retargeting. People will see your advertising when they visit Facebook after leaving your site or demonstrating your designated trigger behaviors. For example, if a person sees your opt-in form on one of your website's pages and then leaves, if you set up a retargeting campaign to be triggered by that action, the visitor should see one of your adverts on another site after leaving yours.

Retargeting aims to repeatedly expose the same offer to a targeted audience so that the fear of missing out is heightened, interest grows, and more individuals take the next step of submitting the form. It's highly successful because many people just need a light reminder or nudge before they act.

Show Your Visitors Your Offer

Once you've gotten people to your website, make sure they notice your opt-in forms. There are literally hundreds of ways to get your opt-in forms in front of visitors who visit your website. Some are subtle, while others are overt, approaching a hard-sell strategy. You must pick which types of opt-in form placements you will utilize to turn visitors into subscribers while avoiding annoying your visitors.

People visit your website to read or watch helpful, meaningful, and timely material. They don't come to be assaulted with opt-in forms that hide the information they seek. Yes, obvious, in-your-face opt-in forms are more likely to build your list faster, but they may irritate some individuals to the point where they never revisit your site. You don't want to lose quality leads; therefore, measure the advantages of increasing the number of subscribers against the user experience visitors desire and expect when they visit your website. Use a variety of positions to find the sweet spot between not bothering visitors and boosting opt-ins.

Tip: A lead magnet or incentive offer is not required for the opt-in form in your sidebar or any other position. Whether or not you add one is entirely up to you and depends on your aims.

Testing and tracking outcomes are required to determine the optimal places for your opt-in forms. Most importantly, recognize that to maximize the success of your opt-in form, you must experiment not only with form design, language, and offers but also with form placement and form type.

Opt-in Form Placements and Types

Opt-in forms can be displayed on your website in a variety of ways. These are known as your form placements. Different placements require different forms; therefore, you must understand what forms are available via your email marketing tool, opt-in form tool, or coding skills. Next, ensure that the placement you wish to utilize will fit and function properly on your website. With that in mind, below are some of the most popular form placements and types to consider incorporating into your website if you're serious about growing your email list.

Sidebar

A sidebar is a content column on some web pages on the left or right side. Sidebar forms are quite popular because they are unobtrusive and simple to construct. Most email marketing systems allow you to construct forms for your site's sidebar—just copy some code and paste it onto your website (e.g., in a text widget in a WordPress site's sidebar) within minutes.

Many visitors expect to see a subscription form in the sidebar of your website, so provide one. You want customers to be able to subscribe to your email marketing list from every page on your website, and a form that appears on all (or many) pages that employ a layout that contains a sidebar is an exceptionally effective approach to achieving this aim.

Pop-Up

Pop-up opt-in forms are incredibly useful, but they may also be annoying. Using pop-up forms carefully and sparingly is the key to having them work for you. A pop-up form appears in front of the browser window on a visitor's screen.

Pop-ups can be set to appear when someone visits your website for the first time, when they visit a specific page, when they click on a specific link, when they scroll to a specified point on a page, or when they try to leave your site.

Your options for configuring when your pop-up appears will vary depending on the program you're using to design your pop-up opt-in forms. The key to success is to ensure that your pop-up forms improve rather than impair the user experience on your website.

Inline

Opt-in forms displayed in a web page's body are known as inline opt-in forms. Your website and coding ability determine the position where an inline form can be displayed. Some WordPress themes, for example, may make it more difficult to display inline forms exactly where you want them to appear than others. Simply copying and pasting text may not function flawlessly, which means you'll need to be able to code to make your forms look right on your live site.

When an inline form is live on your website, the content around it will not be grayed out, as shown here, where the text has been faded to reveal the opt-in form.

Lightbox/Overlay

A lightbox or overlay is an opt-in form that removes distracting elements and can significantly boost the number of subscribers you receive from your opt-in form. When your lightbox or overlay is displayed, all other content in the background is faded away. Visitors must interact with your opt-in form to continue using your website or to proceed to another website.

A visitor activity, such as clicking a link, scrolling, or displaying exit intent, usually triggers a lightbox/overlay opt-in form. Because lightbox/overlay forms necessitate interaction, many marketers find adding a second button to the form extremely effective.

Instead of only having a button that says, "Yes, I want to subscribe" or another call to action, you may also provide a second button that says, "No, I don't want to get awesome tips in my inbox." In other words, rather than simply clicking the X to shut the lightbox/overlay, the visitor is more likely to read the content and choose one of the two available responses. Opt-ins can skyrocket when the second button employs psychologically unattractive copy.

Mobile Pop-Ups

Mobile pop-up opt-in forms appear on mobile devices in front of your web page content. However, be cautious because Google and other search engines dislike anything that prevents web page content from being viewed on mobile devices.

In fact, Google may penalize your site if you employ obtrusive pop-up forms or other forms on your mobile site that may block page content, such as floating headers and footer bars, slide-in forms, and full-screen forms. If your site is punished, Google may send less traffic to it from searches in the future.

You might not want to take the chance if you rely on Google to send traffic to your website (as most do). Instead, utilize inline forms or in-text calls to action to increase mobile opt-ins. Remember to collect opt-ins from your mobile app if you have one.

Landing Page

A landing page is a web page designed to entice visitors to take a certain action known as a conversion. The conversion could be a sale or filling out an opt-in form to gain access to a lead magnet, such as an ebook or webinar. While a landing page is not an opt-in form, it is a vital aspect of growing your email list; therefore, it is necessary to grasp what it is and how to use it.

A landing page can be created with various tools, including Leadpages, Unbounce, Instapage, and MailMunch. Some email marketing systems, such as GetResponse, even provide capabilities for creating landing pages within their program, eliminating the need to purchase a separate product. Of course, if you know how to code, you can construct bespoke landing pages yourself or hire a developer to do it for you. A longer landing page is usually more successful for higher-value conversions.

For example, more messages and details are required to persuade someone to click the button on your landing page to buy a product or arrange a free demo than to click the button and receive a free ebook. Use shorter landing pages for lower-value incentives, like a free checklist or ebook, that swiftly and clearly describe the benefits visitors receive when they enter their email address in the opt-in form.

Improve the Results of Your Online Opt-in Forms

Creating and displaying opt-in forms may not yield immediate results. Don't be concerned: this is extremely common. Remember to direct people to your forms so they may analyze your offerings and decide whether they are more valuable to them than their email addresses. If your results fall short of your expectations, consider expanding your marketing efforts to attract more traffic to your forms (if low traffic is the issue) or modifying your offer (if conversion is the issue).

You can also attempt some of the methods outlined in the rest of this chapter to improve the outcomes of your online opt-in forms. Above all, don't give up!

Show Multiple Opt-In Forms

Displaying several opt-in forms on your website is a simple approach to increasing opt-ins. For example, you can display the same deal on multiple pages throughout your site. You can display multiple offers on the same or separate pages using page-level targeting techniques. Testing is essential in this area. You don't want to overwhelm visitors with opt-in forms, so experiment to discover the sweet spot between many opt-ins and too many forms.

One of the most common errors you may make while creating your email list is assuming that people will find your opt-in form. Give customers multiple methods to find your forms, or you'll miss out on possibilities to increase your list. Consider including a welcome mat form, a sidebar form, an exit-intent pop-up form, and an inline form in your blog entries, for example.

Use CTAs to Direct Visitors to Your Opt-in Forms

Sometimes, you won't be allowed to add a full opt-in form on your website. Instead, utilize calls to action to direct people to your opt-in forms. Include a link with a call to action, for example, next to the submit button in the comment section of your blog entries. Include a call to action in the header of your blog or website and on your social media pages and profiles. You may even include a sign-up form on your Facebook Page.

Don't be scared to ask your current customers and email subscribers to share the link to your opt-in form with others. Create a powerful call to action on your thank-you page or confirmation email after someone submits your opt-in form, urging them to refer their friends to subscribe to your newsletter or download your lead magnet.

One of the most effective areas for e-commerce businesses to incorporate an opt-in call to action message is on the customer's shopping basket page. They're already interested in your brand, so now is the moment to invite them to join your mailing list. However, don't stop there. You should include an opt-in call to action in your abandoned shopping cart advertising. Even if someone isn't ready to buy (and maybe you can alter their mind using abandoned cart email marketing), they could be willing to download your free lead magnet. A sale is preferable, but getting a prospect inside your marketing funnel through an opt-in is preferable to nothing. You can continue to communicate with them via email once they're on your list to convert them from a lead to a customer.

Provide Alternatives

If your offer surpasses your audience's needs, you may need to provide additional options to increase conversions. For example, if visitors are promised a daily email newsletter if they fill out your opt-in form, this may be too much email for some. If your email marketing supplier and opt-in form tool allow, offer numerous subscription options, such as daily, weekly, or monthly.

Another example is allowing visitors to select the frequency of communications from you and the type of messages they will get. You can provide options for receiving instructional or promotional content and communications about certain topics. A health coach may provide the choice of receiving solely content regarding weight loss, exercise, recipes, or low-cholesterol diet suggestions. Assuming the health coach produces enough information to cover all of these issues, providing individuals with this type of option makes them happier and allows the coach to segment the audience. Suppose the coach understands that only a subset of the audience is interested in losing weight. In that case, promotional content connected to weight-loss items can be directed directly to those individuals in the future.

Segment Your Audience and Provide Lead Magnet Options

You can also segment your audience by providing several lead magnet options. For example, a pop-up opt-in form that appears when someone views a given page on your website may offer users the option of downloading one of two ebooks on topics related to but distinct from the page topic. A follow-up email marketing campaign may contain a link to download the second ebook, but you can segment that person depending on their decision when they submit the form. This is useful information for future email marketing campaigns.

Put Your Opt-In Forms to the Test

A/B split tests are the most effective approach to test your opt-in forms and develop the highest-converting forms possible. In its most basic form, an A/B split test necessitates the creation of two distinct variants of the identical opt-in form. You alter one element between the two forms: the element under test. You could, for example, design two identical forms with different headings. Except for one difference, everything is the same. This is important because if you modify more than one element, you won't be able to tell which changed element was responsible for any discrepancies in your results.

If your email marketing service or opt-in form tool supports split testing, you can generate both forms (versions A and B) and publish both to appear randomly in the same location. For example, you could show version A to half of your visitors and version B to the other half. When you have enough data to compare the amount of opt-ins obtained from each form, you can compare them and conclude which form is the winner. Remove the losing form and only show the winning form to all future visitors.

When doing A/B split tests, ensure that your tests are lengthy enough to select a winner confidently. Furthermore, just as scientists repeat studies numerous times before declaring the results reliable, you should repeat your tests at least twice. Rather than displaying one form for a few days and then the second for a few days, ensure you're testing both versions of your form simultaneously. Otherwise, you won't know whether your opt-in form or visitors influenced your findings on your site on different days.

Before Starting Your Email List

To grow your email list, follow the five stages outlined in this chapter: Create relevant offers and effective opt-in forms, direct targeted people to your opt-in forms, display your offers to those visitors, and track performance to improve your outcomes. Remember that there is a step you should take before thinking about online opt-in forms. First, you must ensure that your website appears amazing to foster trust and confidence.

It makes no difference how attractive your opt-in forms are or how well they are displayed if visitors do not trust your website since no one will subscribe if your website fails to satisfy their expectations. Visitors are inclined to assume everything else you offer is low quality if your website is untrustworthy and low quality. Instead, start with a beautiful website and then deliberately build your email list using well-designed and strategically positioned opt-in forms.

PART III

EFFECTIVE EMAIL MARKETING STRATEGIES

CRAFTING COMPELLING EMAIL MESSAGES

E mail marketing is a powerful tool for businesses and organizations to connect with their audience, build relationships, and drive desired actions. However, in a crowded inbox, your email has just a few seconds to capture readers' attention and compel them to open, read, and engage with your message. Crafting compelling email messages is an art that combines the science of data-driven insights with the creativity of persuasive storytelling.

From the enticing subject lines that prompt recipients to click "open" to the persuasive call-to-action (CTA) that drives them to take the desired steps, each element of your email plays a crucial role in its success. We'll delve into the intricacies of each component and provide you with practical tips and best practices that you can implement immediately.

Throughout this guide, we'll emphasize the importance of knowing your audience intimately. Understanding their needs, preferences, pain points, and aspirations is the foundation upon which you'll build your compelling email campaigns. Personalization and relevance are the keys to making your recipients feel valued and understood.

We'll explore the art of concise and engaging copywriting, the strategic placement of visuals, and using social proof to build trust. You'll discover how to create a sense of urgency, leverage scarcity principles, and incorporate the psychology of persuasion into your email messages.

Testing and optimization are crucial aspects of crafting compelling email messages. We'll guide you through A/B testing, analyzing key performance indicators (KPIs), and using data-driven insights to refine your content and strategy. In the ever-evolving world of email marketing, adaptability and continuous improvement are essential.

From the mobile optimization that caters to the on-the-go reader to compliance with email marketing laws, we'll cover all aspects of crafting compelling email messages. We'll also discuss the importance of follow-ups and maintaining a clean and engaged email list to ensure your messages reach their intended audience.

Let's embark on this journey to master the art of crafting compelling email messages and unlock the full potential of your email marketing campaigns.

The Elements of an Email Marketing Message

After you've mastered the fundamentals of copywriting, you may plan your email marketing message. The majority of email marketing communications contain the same set of elements.

You may not always use every element in your messages; some elements may appear in images rather than words. However, if you know how to create each of these components of an email message, you'll be able to produce appealing copy that encourages people to complete your calls to action. When your communications arrive in recipients' inboxes, they have four options: open your message, delete it, ignore it and do nothing, or report it as spam. You should strive for the first answer for every campaign; otherwise, you will waste time and money.

Subject Line

Every email message's subject line is the most important portion. If your subject line fails to attract people's attention and persuade them to open your message, you cannot encourage people to respond to your call to action or meet your objectives. People are more likely to open your message if the subject line describes how they will benefit from opening and seeing the communication. As a result, prioritize advantages over features. Write in the second person and use action-oriented words and phrases. Furthermore, strive to spark recipients' interest by providing something of sufficient perceived worth.

Most importantly, be clear and concise. You should not let innovation and wit take precedence over clarity in your subject lines. According to research, concise subject lines outperform smart subject lines, so tell recipients what they will get and briefly explain why that promise is important to them.

Consider the following example. Instead of sending an email with the subject line "Fitness Tips from the Health Gym," a fitness gym may use a more precise and clear subject line like "25 Proven Exercises You Can Do in Less Than Ten Minutes Each." The first subject line is general and refers to the business, whereas the second one promises something specific that a specific audience could be interested in. It also employs a powerful phrase (proved), which enhances the copy's effect by assuring recipients that the substance of the message is trustworthy. Most importantly, the second subject line employs the second person and communicates both a direct benefit—saving time—and an implicit benefit—losing weight and being fit and healthy.

Here's another example of an email marketing campaign for a freelance writer. Instead of crafting a headline like "Ideas for Weekly Blog Publishing," the freelancer may use content like "If You're Sweating Over Your Weekly Blog Posts, Here's the Solution." The first subject line promises something valuable, while the second subject line is far more effective at piquing recipients' curiosity and motivating them to click. It promises a solution to a specific problem that the freelance writer's target audience of potential business clients is likely to be interested in how to generate enough quality blog content weekly to utilize the power of content marketing.

Text for Inbox Preview

The preview text that your email recipients see following the subject line (if their email inboxes have been configured to allow message previews) is normally between 35 and 140 characters long and is extracted directly from the opening lines of your message content. Many individuals use the preview mode to understand what messages are about before opening them to read them in full. As a result, opening your message's body copy might either assist or damage your open rate.

Fill this little text fragment with benefits because it can provide significant information.-relevant copy that addresses the question on everyone's mind: "What's in it for me if I open this message?" You may not be able to alter this text depending on your email marketing tool; however, if you can, please do so. Most emails sent with email marketing solutions will include wording like "View in a web browser" or other instructions in this preview snippet. That text will not help you achieve your objectives. Ask your email marketing provider how to change this text, and then devote the same amount of effort to it as you do to your subject line. Consider how the preview text appears on all devices.

Headline

You won't use a headline in every email marketing message you send, but when you do, make it a captivating one. For example, if you're creating an email message meant to look like a personal communication and merely contain plain text, putting a title makes little sense. You wouldn't use a headline in a personal letter, so immediately putting one in an email message makes it more promotional and less personal. Headlines work best in messages containing a lot of text, graphics, and videos, which can appear cluttered if no "road signs" take users through the message's road map.

In other words, when people scan your content, the headline and subheadings work together to guide them through it. Most individuals skim communications before reading them completely to ensure they are relevant. Headlines and lists, when combined with visual aids such as images, icons, and videos, can rapidly establish that the message fulfills the promise of the subject line. At that point, recipients will pay more attention to the rest of the material.

A headline is similar to a supplemental or alternative topic line. You enticed readers to open your letter with a compelling subject line, but now you must utilize a compelling headline to persuade them that they are in the correct place and should continue reading.

Because your headlines must be compelling, you should strive to elicit emotions from them. When you can elicit emotions, you instantly establish emotional bonds between your message and its recipients. Most people are motivated by emotions, and most purchases are made partly because of them. Create messages that elicit emotions to increase conversions.

Body Text

It's time to offer more details after you've sparked people's curiosity with an intriguing subject line, preview text, and headline. These are the specifics about your offer for conversion email funnels. Most importantly, your message must fulfill the promise of your subject line or opt-in form by including relevant supporting information.

Begin with the most compelling messages you have. If receivers simply read the first one or two phrases of your message, you must be certain that they will have enough information to judge whether or not the offer is appropriate for them. Following that, offer supporting information to complete your story. Writing in the appropriate style and with the appropriate language for your intended audience is critical. Be conversational, and write as if you're speaking to a single individual rather than a group of email subscribers. Also, don't be scared to deviate from grammar norms. It is more crucial to sound human than to adhere to grammar standards. Use contractions, slang, and sentence fragments if that's the language and style your audience is used to. Rather than being overtly corporate or robotic, personality can make a substantial difference in response rate.

Personalize your messaging as much as possible and use dynamic content to deliver highly targeted offers to the correct people. Personalization and dynamic content, on the other hand, should not be used unless you are sure of the accuracy of your data because personalization errors can cause more harm than benefit. Additionally, avoid overusing personalization in your body copy. Using someone's name once or twice may appear polite, but using it three, four, or more times can be viewed as dishonest. Your message should promote your offer while also establishing trust between recipients and your brand. People are less inclined to trust your brand if the content of your communication is regarded as unauthentic, which can eventually affect conversions.

Of course, you should also describe your offer's benefits in your email message. Benefits sell, but no one will respond to your call to action if they don't know what they'll get in exchange. Avoid writing paragraphs upon paragraphs about features. Instead, present a succinct list that briefly describes the real benefits consumers will gain if they respond to your call to action. Include a list of chapters for an ebook or the expiration date and any exclusions (if any) for a discount code. The importance of brevity cannot be overstated.

Include customer reviews, testimonials, customer success stories, or small case studies in many email marketing messages to back up your claims. Anyone can say that their product will provide benefits, but when an audience sees real people who have the same great results that you advertise in your email message, they are far more likely to respond to your call to action. The key is to keep the social proof section of your emails brief.

Email marketers may frequently build a special email message inside a sequence of communications to share testimonials and client success stories. You could do the same thing or put one testimonial for each message.

Another alternative is to include a variation of this copy directly in the subject line of your email. For example, a message in your email conversion funnel might state, "A $10,000 Google AdWords Success Story You Can Copy." The message's body copy would outline the customer's tale and inform recipients that they might achieve the same outcomes if they took your online course. You have an option. Even better, evaluate your message performance with and without a social proof section to see if it improves conversions.

Call To Action

The call to action in your email marketing communications is crucial because if it does not compel recipients to act, your time and money invested in sending that message will be wasted. The best calls to action are concise and to the point. They clarify exactly what the listener should do, leaving no possibility for misunderstanding. As a result, your call to action should include action phrases and a sense of urgency. Consider this: when do you want people to act? Do you want them to act today, in a month, or anytime they want? You want people to act now if you're aiming to attain a goal (and every email marketing message should have a single, precise objective or purpose). People are more likely to act fast when terms that create a sense of urgency, such as "Act now," or that create a sense of scarcity, such as "Hurry, this offer expires in 23 hours," are used. Make the most of the emotion.

Your call to action should also leave your audience with the impression that there is little or no risk involved. Instead, emphasize the rewards and value they will gain if they respond to the call to action. Create a sense of suspense and excitement, and remove any impediments to completing your call to action. You want the process to be as simple as possible.

Keep the copy on the button short if you include a call to action button in your message that people can click to finish the action. Use a strong verb and an adverb conveying urgency, such as "now." Also, in your button copy, use the first person. In this scenario, the first individual does not relate to you or your company.

It is a reference to the email recipient. Use call-to-action button wording that says something like, "I Want My Free Ebook," "Send My Checklist Now," or "Get My Coupon Code Now." This personalizes the activity and may enhance conversion rates.

Footer

The footer of your website, similar to the footer of a document, is frequently generated automatically by your email marketing provider based on information in your account. The sender's firm name, address, and phone number are typically included in the footer. It's also a good idea to include your company's website URL in the footer, as well as your social media account icons (be sure these are live links so people can click to follow you) and your logo (if it isn't already in the message's header). In the footer, include an unsubscribe link that allows individuals to unsubscribe from your list in one simple step.

Writing Various Styles of Email Marketing Messages

You can and should be creative with the email marketing messages you send, but most of them will fall into one of three categories: one-time campaigns, automated sequences, or newsletters. As detailed in the rest of this chapter, each form of message has a somewhat different purpose.

One-time Ad Hoc or Automated Campaigns

One-time email marketing campaigns are single-message campaigns that can be sent ad hoc (on an as-needed or unscheduled basis) or automatically, such as autoresponder programs. You can use an ad hoc campaign (or a one-time campaign) to send a single promotional or informational email message to a section of your email marketing list or your complete list.

For example, a promotional ad hoc campaign could promote a new blog post or a 24-hour offer. A promotional call to action would not be included in an informational ad hoc campaign. Instead, it would offer helpful, meaningful, and relevant information to develop a relationship with receivers, eventually leading to brand trust, purchases, and loyalty. Be brief and appeal to emotional triggers while writing this type of letter.

Use the email marketing message elements discussed in this chapter in your body content to create a message your target audience will want to receive, open, read, and respond to by following your call to action.

Newsletters

Newsletters are distributed exclusively for informative purposes, though promotional messages may be included. Just keep promotional messaging to a minimum in your newsletters, or you'll be delivering promotions disguised as newsletters instead of useful ones. Your target audience will not fall for it, and they will not enjoy it. Your unsubscribe rate will increase if your newsletters become promotional messages.

Newsletters are often distributed daily, weekly, bimonthly, or monthly. You can incorporate original content in your emails by writing a complete article (or numerous pieces) just for your readers that will not be published or shared elsewhere. If you wish, you can send your latest blog content via your newsletter. Write brief summaries of your most recent blog entries and provide links to them in your emails so that recipients may click through to read the complete posts on your website.

Another approach is to distribute curated material via your newsletters. To accomplish this, search the web for exceptional content that your target audience is likely to love and include links to it and descriptions of each in your newsletters. In your emails, you might also blend some of these sorts of material (original articles, linked blog pieces, and curated information).

Most importantly, avoid sending newsletters that exclusively contain company information. People are interested in how your company, products, and services may make their lives better, easier, or happier. Your newsletter copy should be useful and meaningful to your audience, with far more content that prioritizes their wants and needs and far less content that prioritizes your company's wants and needs (for example, talking about the award you received or the retreat your team attended). It's beautiful to give customers a peek behind the scenes of your firm to make it feel more human, but use caution and limit this type of content to a few pages.

Consider your reason for sending a newsletter. Is it to increase brand trust? Is it to establish yourself as a subject matter expert? Is it to increase the sale of goods or services? The content of your mailings may differ depending on your responses. Identify your purpose, as with other email marketing projects, and then write messages (in this case, newsletters) that align with it.

Improving Your Copy and Email Marketing Outcomes

One thing is clear in email marketing: anything can and should be tested. That implies you should test all your message elements to see which copy produces the best results. Create A/B split tests and try different subject lines, preview excerpts, headings, body content, and calls to action. Combine these efforts with message design element testing to determine the best-converting copy and overall design.

COLD EMAIL MARKETING

In today's digital age, where inboxes are bustling personal, professional, and promotional communications hubs, standing out becomes a challenge. One might ponder why, in such a cluttered space, one should consider cold emailing a marketing strategy. The answer is simple: When executed correctly, cold emails can unlock doors to potential clients, partnerships, and opportunities you might not have imagined.

What is Cold Email Marketing?

Cold email marketing refers to the practice of sending an unsolicited email to a potential client, partner, or professional connection without prior contact. Think of it as the digital equivalent of a cold call. But, unlike its telephonic counterpart, a cold email allows the recipient to respond at their own pace, which can lead to more thoughtful and positive interactions.

Why are Cold Emails Crucial for Business Development?

- **Reaching Out to New Audiences:** Cold emails allow businesses to reach out to a whole new audience segment that might not be aware of their products or services. It's a proactive approach rather than waiting for potential clients to discover you.
- **Cost-Effective:** Compared to traditional advertising methods or even digital ad campaigns, cold emailing is relatively inexpensive. With a

well-maintained email list and a compelling message, the ROI can be substantial.

- **Personal Touch:** Unlike mass advertisements, cold emails can be tailored and personalized for each recipient. This personal touch can lead to higher engagement rates.
- **Building Professional Relationships:** Cold emails aren't just for sales. They can be a powerful tool for establishing partnerships, getting press coverage, or even seeking mentorship.

Before we delve deep into the nuances of crafting that perfect cold email, understanding compliance, and mastering the art of engagement, it's essential to understand that cold emailing isn't about bombarding strangers with sales pitches. It's about starting genuine conversations, nurturing relationships, and providing value.

In the forthcoming sections, we will equip you with the tools, strategies, and insights to make cold emailing a potent weapon in your marketing arsenal. Whether you're a seasoned marketer or a business owner just venturing into the world of cold email marketing, a trove of knowledge is waiting to be unearthed.

The Art of the Cold Email

Cold emailing, at its core, is about building connections. It's an exercise in communication where clarity meets persuasion, and relevance converges with value. But to truly master this art, we need to dissect its components, understanding each element's significance and role in the grand tapestry of engagement.

Defining Your Objective

Every communication has a purpose, a reason that justifies its existence. This reason translates to your email's objective in the world of cold emailing. Here, we'll delve deep into the significance of defining an objective, the different types you might encounter, and the pitfalls of a multi-faceted approach.

Why Objectives Matter

An email without a precise aim is like an arrow shot in the dark, lacking direction and focus.

- **Clarity of Message:** Knowing your objective aids in formulating a crisp and clear message. It offers guidance on what to include and, equally important, what to exclude.
- **Guide to Action:** A clear objective provides direction for the email's call to action. It answers the "What next?" for the reader.
- **Measuring Success:** With a defined objective, you have a metric or outcome against which to measure the email's effectiveness. Whether it's the number of responses, scheduled meetings, or link clicks, your objective helps set the benchmark.

Types of Objectives

Cold emails can serve various purposes. While the end game might be conversion or collaboration, the immediate objective can vary.

- **Introducing a Product/Service:** The email aims to inform the recipient of a new offering. The tone is informative, possibly with a hint of excitement.
- **Setting Up a Meeting or Call:** The objective is to get some time from the recipient. This type of email focuses on proposing value or benefits that a discussion can bring about.

115

- **Seeking Advice or Mentorship:** A humbler approach, where the emailer is reaching out to gain insights, feedback, or guidance from the recipient.
- **Building a Partnership or Collaboration:** The focus here is mutual growth. The email highlights potential synergies between both parties.

Keeping It Singular

While killing two birds with one stone is tempting, simplicity is critical in cold emailing.

- **Avoiding Confusion:** Multiple objectives can muddle the email's message, leading to confusion or a lack of clear action for the recipient.
- **Prioritizing Importance:** If everything is a priority, then nothing is. Focusing on a single objective underlines its importance, driving the recipient's attention to that particular action or outcome.
- **Crafting Tailored Follow-Ups:** With a singular objective, follow-ups become easier to tailor. They can be specifically crafted around the primary goal of the original email, be it to nudge for a response, provide additional information, or address any queries.

Crafting an effective cold email is akin to sculpting—each chisel, each word, and each intent brings it closer to its final form. The objective is the vision, the guiding light that shapes the email's direction and purpose. As we proceed, remember that this foundational step will determine the trajectory of your cold email campaigns.

Researching the Recipient

The efficacy of cold emailing hinges upon its ability to resonate with the recipient. A tailored, relevant message that speaks directly to its reader is more likely to be opened, read, and acted upon. This is why researching the recipient isn't merely a recommended step—it's foundational.

Why Research is Pivotal

Research allows you to tailor your email, ensuring it's not just another generic message lost in the vast sea of an inbox. When you take the time to understand the person you're reaching out to, it reflects respect and signals that you're genuinely interested in building a meaningful connection.

Sources of Research

- **Professional Platforms:** Websites like LinkedIn provide a wealth of information about a person's professional background, achievements, endorsements, and more.
- **Company Websites:** Delve into the "About Us" or "Team" sections. This can give you insights into the recipient's role, contributions, and even the company's ethos and objectives.
- **Social Media:** Twitter, Instagram, or even personal blogs can provide more informal insights, giving you a rounded perspective about personal interests, recent activities, and viewpoints.
- **Publications:** Articles, interviews, or press releases can provide recent achievements, project involvements, or company directions.

Using Your Findings

- **Tailoring the Tone:** If you find out your recipient is more laid-back from their social media, perhaps a more conversational tone might work. Conversely, a formal tone might be more appropriate for high-level executives.

- **Referencing Shared Connections or Interests:** Mentioning a mutual acquaintance or referencing a shared interest can be an effective icebreaker.

- **Aligning Objectives:** If you've discovered that the recipient has recently been involved in a project that aligns with your product or service, highlight this alignment in your pitch.

- **Avoiding Overfamiliarity:** While personalization is key, striking a balance is crucial. You don't want to come off as invasive or creepy by mentioning too many personal details.

Regularly Updating Your Database

- **The Fluidity of Information:** People change roles, companies pivot directions, and industries evolve. What was relevant a year ago might not be today.

- **Scheduling Regular Checks:** Especially if you're reaching out to a list over an extended period, periodically update your information to ensure you're always sending out relevant content.

Research, in essence, is the backbone of effective cold emailing. It bridges the gap between a stranger's unsolicited message and a tailored, insightful proposal that prompts the recipient to think, "This email was meant for me." We harness this research to craft a compelling narrative as we move forward.

Structuring a Cold Email: The Beginning, Middle, and End

The composition of a cold email can be likened to that of a classic story arc. It requires a captivating introduction to draw readers in, a substantive middle that delivers key messages, and a conclusion that prompts action. Each component has its role, and when executed properly, they harmoniously guide the recipient through the email's narrative.

The Beginning: Crafting a Strong Entrance

- **The First Impression:** Just as the opening line of a book can determine if you'll turn the page, the beginning of your email determines if the reader will continue. It's your chance to capture attention and spark interest.

- **Establishing a Connection:** The goal here isn't just to introduce yourself but to find a common point of interest. Perhaps it's a mutual contact, a shared experience, or simply appreciation for the recipient's work. *Example:* "I recently came across your insightful piece on digital marketing trends in 'XYZ Magazine,' and it really resonated with me."

- **Keep It Brief:** Respect the recipient's time. A concise yet effective introduction lays a solid foundation without overwhelming the reader.

The Middle: Delivering Your Core Message

- **Clarity and Purpose:** Clearly articulate the purpose of your email. Why are you reaching out? What value or proposition are you bringing to the table? *Example:* "Given your expertise in digital marketing and my experience with AI-driven marketing tools, I believe there's potential for a mutually beneficial collaboration."

- **Alignment with Recipient's Interests:** Ensure that your message aligns with what might interest or benefit the recipient. This is where your prior research plays a pivotal role. *Example:* "Considering your company's recent expansion into e-commerce, our AI-driven marketing tool could help optimize your online campaigns."
- **Anticipate Questions:** Address the recipient's potential questions or concerns, offering solutions or further points of contact for clarity.

The End: Prompting Action with a Clear Call-to-Action (CTA)

- **Define the Next Steps:** Guide the recipient on what you want them to do next. Be specific in your ask, whether it's a phone call, meeting, or checking out a linked resource. *Example:* "Would you be available for a brief call next Tuesday to discuss how we could potentially collaborate?"
- **Offer Flexibility:** While you should propose a specific CTA, also provide room for alternatives. This gives the recipient a sense of control and choice. *Example:* "If next Tuesday doesn't work for you, please let me know a time that suits your schedule."
- **Express Gratitude:** Always end with a note of thanks, appreciating the recipient's time and consideration. This leaves a positive impression and reinforces the human touch in your communication.

Crafting an effective cold email requires thoughtful structure. With the right balance of personal connection, clear messaging, and actionable next steps, you can transform a cold outreach into a warm conversation, paving the way for meaningful professional relationships.

Strategies for Improving Cold Email Open Rates

Regardless of how well-crafted, cold emails lose their purpose if they remain unopened. The open rate of your email campaign is a critical metric in determining the initial success of your outreach. Let's delve deep into the strategies that can significantly boost these rates, ensuring your message doesn't just reach the inbox but also captures attention.

Crafting an Irresistible Subject Line

The subject line is your first impression. It's the deciding factor between your email being opened or trashed.

- **Keep it Short and Sweet:** Aim for 50 characters or less. This ensures that the subject line is fully visible, even on mobile devices.
- **Evoke Curiosity:** Subject lines like "A solution you've been looking for?" or "Heard about the latest in [industry trend]?" can pique interest.
- **Personalize:** Including the recipient's name or referencing something specific to them can increase open rates. For example, "John, an exclusive offer for you."
- **Avoid SPAM Triggers:** Words like "Free," "Buy now," or "Urgent" can land your email in the spam folder.

The Role of Timing: When to Send Your Cold Emails

When you send your email, it can be just as crucial as what's inside it.

- **Avoid Mondays:** It's typically the day when inboxes are the most cluttered.
- **Midweek Magic:** Studies have shown that Tuesday, Wednesday, and Thursday see higher open rates.

- **Time it Right:** Sending emails during the recipient's working hours increases visibility. If you're targeting multiple time zones, consider scheduling tools.

The Power of Follow-Ups: How Persistence Pays Off

Sometimes, a single email might get lost in the shuffle. Following up can drastically increase your chances of getting noticed.

- **Don't Be Overly Persistent:** Give them a week before sending a follow-up. Bombarding them with daily reminders can come off as aggressive.
- **Reference the Previous Email:** Start your follow-up by referencing your previous message. It helps in continuity.
- **Limit the Number:** While follow-ups are effective, there should be a cap. It might be time to move on if you haven't received a response after 2 or 3 follow-ups.

A/B Testing for Cold Emails: Tweaking for Better Results

Sometimes, minor tweaks can yield significant results. A/B testing lets you understand what works best.

- **Elements to Test:** From subject lines and email content to call-to-actions and sending times, almost everything can be A/B tested.
- **Analyze and Iterate:** Once you have the results, analyze the differences. Implement the winning strategies in future campaigns.

Overcoming Common Pitfalls and Objections

Cold emailing isn't without its challenges. It's essential to anticipate potential objections and be prepared to address them.

- **Relevance Issues:** Ensure that your email is sent to the right person in the organization.
- **Value Proposition:** Be clear about what you're offering and how it can benefit the recipient.
- **Transparency:** If the recipient has questions or doubts about your product, service, or intent, address them candidly.

Improving cold email open rates is a combination of art and science. While crafting a compelling message is an art, understanding and analyzing the metrics, tweaking strategies, and being adaptable is the science. Marrying the two can lead to cold emailing success.

99+ EMAIL TEMPLATES

Efficiency and effectiveness are at the heart of any successful email marketing campaign. Email templates serve both of these purposes. They provide a standardized format that can be swiftly customized for various needs, ensuring consistency in branding and messaging. Additionally, with a template, the marketer doesn't have to start from scratch every time, saving time and effort.

Moreover, templates are designed based on tried-and-tested formats, increasing the chances of garnering higher open rates, engagement, and conversions. They integrate the best practices of email marketing, ensuring the final output adheres to standards that are proven to work. This includes clear calls to action, engaging visuals, and concise content that captures attention.

Customizing Templates for Your Brand Voice

While templates offer a solid foundation, it's pivotal that businesses don't lose their unique voice amidst the standardization. The best email templates are those that can be effortlessly molded to reflect a brand's individual personality. This means adjusting colors to match brand guidelines, tweaking language to sound like 'you,' and incorporating specific imagery or graphics that resonate with your company's ethos. A good template is like clay: it gives you a starting shape, but it's malleable enough to be transformed into a unique sculpture.

It's essential to strike a balance. Over-customization can defeat the purpose of using a template and under-customization can make the email feel impersonal. The goal is to make the recipient feel the message was crafted just for them, even though it was built on a template.

Best Practices for Template Use

Using templates effectively demands an understanding of some best practices:

- **Stay Updated:** Like everything in the digital world, email marketing trends evolve. Ensure your templates remain contemporary, aligning with both current design trends and the latest in user experience best practices.
- **Segmentation:** One template won't fit all. You might need several templates depending on your target demographics and the message's purpose. Segment your audience and tailor your templates accordingly.
- **Test Regularly:** Even the best templates can benefit from A/B testing. Regularly test different versions of your emails to understand what resonates best with your audience.
- **Maintain Brand Consistency:** As mentioned earlier, customization is key. But while doing so, always ensure the core elements like logo placement, color schemes, and fonts remain consistent with your brand guidelines.

Hence, it's safe to say that email templates are invaluable tools in a marketer's arsenal. They streamline the email creation process, ensure brand consistency, and incorporate the industry's best practices. However, the real magic happens when these templates are thoughtfully customized to resonate deeply with the intended audience, striking the right chord between efficiency and personal touch.

PART I

GENERAL EMAIL MARKETING TEMPLATES

Welcome Emails

Welcome emails are the first point of official communication between your brand and a new subscriber or customer. They set the tone for your future interactions and have the power to build trust, establish your brand's voice, and promote further engagement.

Why Welcome Emails Matter

- **First Impressions Count:** First impressions are pivotal in face-to-face interactions. A well-crafted welcome email can set the stage for a strong, long-term relationship with your subscribers.
- **High Open Rates:** Welcome emails typically have 4x higher open rates and 5x higher click-through rates than regular marketing emails.
- **Immediate Engagement:** They provide an immediate touchpoint with subscribers when your brand is still fresh in their minds.
- **Opportunity to Educate:** You can introduce your brand's story, values, and what the subscriber can expect in terms of content and frequency.
- **Trust Building:** They offer a chance to reinforce your subscriber's decision by signing up or purchasing.

Templates

V1. E-commerce Welcome Email (#001)

Welcome to [Brand Name] - Here's a little gift for you!

Hello [First Name],

Welcome to the [Brand Name] family! We're thrilled to have you on board.

At [Brand Name], we believe in [briefly describe the brand's mission, e.g., "providing sustainable, high-quality fashion that makes you feel and look amazing."]

For being awesome, here's a **10% discount** on your first order: **WELCOME10**

Why shop with us?

- [Benefit 1: e.g., "Sustainably sourced materials"]
- [Benefit 2: e.g., "Unique designs you won't find elsewhere"]
- [Benefit 3: e.g., "Hassle-free returns and exchanges"]

Ready to start shopping? [Shop Now]

Stay stylish,

The [Brand Name] Team

V2. Newsletter Subscription Welcome Email (#002)

You're In! Welcome to [Newsletter Name].

Hi [First Name],

You've just unlocked a world of insights with [Newsletter Name]!

Here's what you can expect:

- Weekly insights straight to your inbox every [specific day, e.g., "Thursday morning"].
- Deep dives into [topics your newsletter covers, e.g., "latest tech trends, innovative startups, and actionable business insights"].

- Exclusive interviews with industry leaders

As a token of appreciation, here's an article that our readers have absolutely loved: [Link to a popular article or resource]

Got suggestions or topics you're curious about? Hit reply and let us know!

Cheers to growth and knowledge!

[Your Name or Brand Name]

V3. Service or SaaS Platform Welcome Email (#003)

[First Name], Get Started with [Service Name]!

Hello [First Name],

Thank you for choosing [Service Name]. Your journey to [what your service achieves, e.g., "streamlining team collaboration"] begins here.

Quick Steps to Get Started:

- Set up your profile: [Profile Setup Link]
- Join our introductory webinar: [Webinar Link]
- Explore our user guide: [User Guide Link]

Why users love [Service Name]:

- [Feature/Benefit 1: e.g., "Real-time collaboration with team members"]
- [Feature/Benefit 2: e.g., "Easily integrate with tools you already use"]
- [Feature/Benefit 3: e.g., "24/7 customer support"]

Need assistance or have questions? Our support team is here to help: [Support Link or Email]

Welcome aboard, and here's to achieving [specific goal, e.g., "seamless collaboration"] together!

Warm regards,

The [Service Name] Team

First Purchase Thank You Email

The first purchase a customer makes from your business is a pivotal moment. It affirms trust and is a potential starting point for lasting customer loyalty. A well-crafted "First Purchase Thank You Email" can enhance this experience, solidify your brand's reputation, and encourage future interactions.

Why Send a First Purchase Thank You Email?

- **Building Relationships:** It personalizes the buying experience. People like to feel appreciated, and a simple 'thank you' goes a long way.
- **Promoting Brand Loyalty:** It's the first step in converting a one-time buyer into a loyal customer.
- **Opportunity for Upselling:** You can promote other products by adding relevant product recommendations.
- **Gathering Feedback:** It's an opportunity to ask the customer about their shopping experience, helping you improve.

Templates

V1. *Friendly & Appreciative* (#004)

Welcome to [Your Brand] Family! Thanks for Your First Purchase

Hello [Customer's First Name],

We're absolutely thrilled to see you here!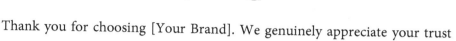

Thank you for choosing [Your Brand]. We genuinely appreciate your trust and are committed to ensuring you love your new [product name].

A few things to note:

- Your order #[Order Number] is being processed and will be shipped soon.
- Need any assistance or have questions? Our friendly support team is here for you. Just hit reply!
- Stay tuned for exclusive deals and brand stories – we're sure you'll love them.

Thanks again, [Customer's First Name]. Here's to the beginning of a fantastic journey together!

Warmly,

[Your Name/Your Brand Team]

V2. *Enthusiastic & Engaging* (#005)

You Did It, [Customer's First Name]! Your First [Your Brand] Purchase is Confirmed

Hey [Customer's First Name],

High-five! You've just unlocked a world of awesomeness with your first purchase at [Your Brand]. We bet you're going to adore your new [product name].

While you eagerly await your package, here's what's happening behind the scenes:

- Our team is dancing a little jig because you chose us.
- Your [product name] is getting all dressed up and ready for its journey to you.
- We're prepping some fantastic surprises for our family members – yup, that includes you!

Got any questions or just want to chat about your purchase? Slide into our DMs or shoot us an email. We're all ears!

Cheers to more delightful experiences, [Customer's First Name]!

Stay fab,

[Your Name/Your Brand Team]

Download or Signup Thank You Email

A "Download or Signup Thank You Email" is an automated message sent to users immediately after they've taken an action, such as downloading a resource (like an e-book or a white paper) or signing up for a service (like a newsletter or a free trial). It's an integral touchpoint in the user's journey, serving both as a confirmation of the action they've taken and an opportunity to engage them further.

Templates

V1. Simple Thank You (#006)

Welcome, and Thanks for Signing Up!

Hello [First Name],

Thank you for signing up and downloading [Product/Resource Name]!

We're thrilled to have you onboard. Here's a quick link to access your [Product/Resource Name] anytime: [Link to Product/Resource]

Looking for more? Check out our [Blog/Resource Center/Forum/etc.] for the latest updates and insights.

Stay connected!

Warm regards,

[Your Name/Your Company Name]

V2. Offer Additional Value (#007)

Your Download is Ready + A Special Bonus!

Hey [First Name],

Your download for [Product/Resource Name] is complete! Access it here: [Link to Product/Resource]

As a token of our appreciation, we've also included a bonus for you: [Bonus Resource Name]. We believe it will complement your recent download and add even more value.

Grab your bonus here: [Link to Bonus Resource]

Thanks for being awesome!

Cheers,

[Your Name/Your Company Name]

V3. Engage & Interact (#008)

[First Name], Thank You for Your Download! How Can We Assist You Further?

Hi [First Name],

First, THANK YOU for downloading [Product/Resource Name]. Access your content anytime here: [Link to Product/Resource]

We're on a mission to provide the best experience for our community. So, we'd love to hear from you:

- How did you find us?
- What topics or resources would you like to see in the future?
- Any feedback on the download?

Hit reply and let us know. Your insights are invaluable!

Until next time,

[Your Name/Your Company Name]

Welcome After Free Trial Email

The "Welcome After Free Trial Email" is an essential communication tool for businesses offering trial periods for their products or services. This email is a transition point between the user's trial experience and their potential journey as a paying customer. It aims to engage, retain, and convert trial users by highlighting the benefits they've experienced and what they stand to gain as full-fledged members or subscribers.

A well-crafted "Welcome After Free Trial Email" not only serves as a bridge between the trial and potential conversion phases but also establishes a continued relationship with the user. Businesses can increase their chances of retaining users and expanding their customer base by effectively combining gratitude, personalized messaging, clear CTAs, and added incentives.

Templates

V1. The Encouraging Welcome (#009)

Your Free Trial Has Ended – Let's Continue The Journey!

Dear [First Name],

We noticed you recently wrapped up your free trial with [Your Product/Service]. How did it go?

As you step into the next phase, we want to ensure your experience is smooth and rewarding. Here's what you can expect now:

- **Full Access:** Dive deep into all the premium features you've just touched upon.
- **Expert Tips:** Weekly insights to make the most of [Your Product/Service]

- **24/7 Support:** We're always here to assist you round the clock.

Ready to take the plunge? **Upgrade now** and continue your journey with us.

Cheers to new beginnings,

[Your Company Name]

V2. *The Exclusive Offer Welcome* (#010)

A Little Thank You for Trying Us Out – Exclusive Offer Inside!

Hi [First Name],

Your free trial might have ended, but our commitment to your success has just begun. As a token of our appreciation for giving [Your Product/Service] a shot, we're offering you an exclusive **20% discount** on your first month.

Use code: THANKYOU20.

Why stay with us?

- **Unlimited Access:** No restrictions, just unlimited potential.
- **Community Benefits:** Join forums, webinars, and exclusive events.
- **Continual Upgrades:** We're always evolving for you.

This offer is valid for the next 48 hours, so don't wait too long!

Warm regards,

[Your Company Name]

V3. The Feedback-Focused Welcome (#011)

How Was Your Experience, [First Name]?

Hello [First Name],

Your free trial with [Your Product/Service] has concluded, and we're eager to hear your thoughts! Feedback from users like you helps us create a more tailored experience for all.

Quick Feedback Survey *(takes only 2 minutes)*

Whether you decide to continue with us or take a different path, we genuinely value and appreciate the time you spent exploring our platform.

If you loved your trial and wish to continue, we've made the next steps super simple. Click below to pick up right where you left off:

Continue with [Your Product/Service]

Thank you for trying us; we hope to see you again!

Best wishes,

[Your Company Name]

Promotional Emails

Promotional emails are messages sent to promote products, services, events, or offers to elicit a specific action from the recipient, such as making a purchase, signing up for an event, or redeeming a discount.

Primary Roles of Promotional Emails

- **Drive Sales and Revenue**: Promotional emails can directly impact a business's bottom line by prompting recipients to make a purchase.

- **Increase Brand Awareness**: Even if a recipient doesn't purchase immediately, consistently seeing promotional content can keep a brand top-of-mind for future buying decisions.
- **Introduce New Products or Services**: These emails help companies launch and gain traction for new offerings.
- **Move Inventory**: Promotions can help clear out older stock, making room for new products.
- **Drive Traffic**: Whether it's to a physical store or a website, promotional emails can increase foot and web traffic.
- **Enhance Customer Loyalty**: Exclusive promotions for email subscribers can make them feel valued, leading to increased brand loyalty.

Potential Challenges

- **Over-saturation**: If recipients receive too many promotional emails, they may unsubscribe or mark emails as spam.
- **Irrelevance**: Sending offers that aren't pertinent can lead to disengagement.
- **Poor Timing**: Promotions that aren't timely or are sent at odd hours can be less effective.

Templates

V1. New Product Launch (#012)

Introducing [Product Name] - The Future Is Here!

Hi [First Name],

We're thrilled to announce the launch of our brand new [Product Name]!

Why you'll love [Product Name]:

- [Feature 1]
- [Feature 2]
- [Feature 3]

Special Offer: Be one of the first to get your hands on [Product Name] and enjoy [discount amount]% off for a limited time.

[CTA: Shop Now]

Cheers to innovation,

[Your Company Name]

V2. Seasonal Sale (#013)

Dive into our Summer Sale - Up to 50% Off!

Hey [First Name],

The temperatures are rising, and so are the discounts at [Your Company Name]!

Save up to 50% on your favorite items this summer.

Hurry, sale ends [End Date]!

[CTA: Browse the Sale]

Stay cool and stylish,

[Your Company Name]

V3. *Exclusive Member Offer* (#014)

Because You're Special: Exclusive Offer Inside!

Hello [First Name],

As a token of our appreciation for being a loyal member, we've got an exclusive offer just for you.

Get [discount amount]% off your next purchase with the code: **SPECIALMEMBER**

This offer is valid until [End Date], so don't miss out!

[CTA: Redeem Your Offer]

Thank you for choosing us,

[Your Company Name]

V4. *Cart Abandonment Reminder* (#015)

Oops! Did You Forget Something?

Hey [First Name],

We noticed you left some items in your cart. We don't want you to miss out!

For a limited time, enjoy [discount amount]% off your cart with the code: **LEFTBEHIND**

[CTA: Complete Your Purchase]

Happy shopping,

[Your Company Name]

V5. Limited Time Flash Sale (#016)

Flash Sale Alert: Only 24 Hours to Save!

Hello [First Name],

Surprise! We're having a 24-hour flash sale, and you're invited.

Save [discount amount]% on select items - but act fast; these deals won't last long!

The sale ends at [End Time].

[CTA: Shop the Flash Sale]

Tick tock,

[Your Company Name]

Transactional Emails

Transactional emails are automated messages sent to individuals based on their interactions or transactions with a website, service, or application. Unlike promotional emails that aim to market or sell, transactional emails provide information that recipients expect due to a specific action they've taken.

Roles of Transactional Emails

- **Informational**: At its core, the main purpose of transactional emails is to inform users about their interactions. This might include account registration confirmations, order receipts, shipping notifications, password resets, and more.

- **Engagement & Trust Building**: Transactional emails have an open rate that is generally much higher than promotional emails. Due to their anticipated and often vital content, they create an opportunity for businesses to engage users, reinforce branding, and build trust.

- **Customer Retention & Upselling**: While the primary goal isn't sales, strategic marketers can use transactional emails as a platform for subtle upselling or cross-selling. For example, an order confirmation email can also highlight related products.

- **Feedback & Data Collection**: Many businesses use transactional emails to solicit feedback. A post-purchase email might include a request for a product review or a survey about the shopping experience.

- **Compliance & Legal**: Transactional emails often serve legal or compliance purposes. For instance, invoices, account statements, and terms of service updates are often delivered via transactional emails.

- **User Re-engagement**: Sometimes, transactional emails serve as reminders that can prompt users to re-engage with a platform, like "abandoned cart" emails in e-commerce, which remind users of products they've left behind.

- **Security & Verification**: Transactional emails play a pivotal role in online security. Email verifications and two-factor authentication prompts are examples where transactional emails contribute to safeguarding user data.

Templates

V1. Order Confirmation (#017)

Order Confirmation: Thank you for your purchase, [First Name]!

Hello [First Name],

Thank you for your order! We're currently processing the following items for you:

[Order Details]

Estimated delivery: [Date]

Track your order here: [Tracking Link]

Questions? Contact our customer service team at [support email/phone number].

Thank you for shopping with [Brand Name]!

Best,

[Your Brand Name]

V2. Order Delivery Email (#018)

Your [Brand Name] order has been delivered!

Hello [First Name],

We're excited to let you know that your order #[Order Number] has been delivered!

[Order Details]

We hope everything is as you expected. Enjoy your purchase!

Have questions or concerns? Contact our support at [support email/phone number].

Thank you for choosing [Brand Name].

Best wishes,

[Your Brand Name]

V3. *Invoice Email* (#019)

Invoice for your recent [Brand Name] purchase

Hello [First Name],

Thank you for your order. Please find your invoice details below:

Invoice Number: [Invoice Number]

Order Number: [Order Number]

Date: [Date]

Total Amount: [Amount]

[Brief Order Details or link to a detailed invoice]

For payment methods and details, click here: [Payment Link]

Should you have any queries regarding this invoice, please reach out to our finance team at [finance email].

Thank you for shopping with [Brand Name].

Best regards,

[Your Brand Name]

V4. Refund or Cancellation Confirmation Email (#020)

Refund/Cancellation Confirmation for your [Brand Name] Order

Hello [First Name],

We're writing to confirm that we have processed the refund/cancellation for your order #[Order Number].

Details:

[Order Details]

Refund Amount: [Amount]

The refund should reflect in your account within [X days], depending on your bank's processing time. If you don't see it by then, please reach out to your bank or contact us at [support email/phone number].

We apologize for any inconvenience and appreciate your understanding. We hope to serve you again in the future.

Thank you for choosing [Brand Name].

Warm regards,

[Your Brand Name]

V5. Password Reset (#021)

Password Reset Request for [Brand Name]

Hello [First Name],

We received a request to reset the password for your [Brand Name] account.

Reset your password: [Reset Link]

If you did not request this change, please contact us immediately at [support email/phone number].

Stay safe,

[Your Brand Name]

V6. *Feedback Request* (#022)

We'd love to hear from you, [First Name]!

Hello [First Name],

Thank you for choosing [Brand Name]! We hope you're enjoying [Product/Service].

We always strive to improve and would love to hear your thoughts. Would you mind taking a quick survey?

Provide feedback: [Survey Link]

Your insights are invaluable. Thank you for being a part of our journey!

Warm regards,

[Your Brand Name]

Newsletters and Content Updates

Newsletters and content updates are integral components of email marketing strategies. Let's delve into their significance, benefits, and best practices.

Role of Newsletters and Content Updates in Email Marketing:

Audience Engagement

- **Regular Touchpoint:** Newsletters provide a consistent touchpoint with subscribers, ensuring your brand remains top-of-mind.
- **Builds Community:** Regular updates help foster a sense of community, making subscribers feel a part of your brand's journey.

Content Distribution

- **Broaden Reach:** They offer a platform to share new blog posts, articles, videos, and other content types directly with a vested audience.
- **Drive Traffic:** You drive traffic back to your website or platform by highlighting recent content.

Direct Sales & Promotions

- **Highlight Products/Services:** Newsletters can showcase new products, bestsellers, or specific promotions.
- **Increase ROI:** With targeted promotions, exclusive discounts, or tailored content, newsletters can directly boost sales.

Education & Value Addition

- **Informative Content:** Share industry news, trends, tutorials, or insights that provide value to readers.

- **Establish Authority:** Over time, consistently delivering valuable content establishes your brand as a thought leader in the space.

Feedback & Data Collection

- **Surveys & Polls:** Include these in newsletters to gather feedback or insights about your audience.
- **Data-Driven Decisions:** Open rates, click-through rates, and other metrics can guide content and strategy decisions.

Personalization & Segmentation

- **Targeted Content:** Based on user behavior, preferences, or past interactions, deliver content that resonates.
- **Enhanced Relevance:** Segmented newsletters lead to better engagement and fewer unsubscribes because they're more relevant to the reader.

Brand Building & Storytelling

- **Brand Voice & Personality:** Newsletters convey your brand's voice, values, and persona.
- **Story Arcs:** Over multiple editions, create narratives around campaigns, products, or corporate stories.

Benefits

- **Cost-Effective:** Email marketing, especially newsletters, is one of the most cost-effective marketing strategies with a high ROI.
- **Direct Access:** Reach audiences directly in their inbox, a personal space, making the interaction more intimate.
- **Flexibility:** Adapt content, design, frequency, and segmentation easily based on insights and changing business goals.

- **Measurable:** Analytics can help you understand what's working and what isn't, allowing for constant optimization.

Newsletters and content updates are not just tools for sharing information. When executed correctly, they are powerful mechanisms for driving engagement, sales, brand loyalty, and much more. A strategic approach to these tools can significantly amplify a brand's digital marketing efforts.

Templates

V1. Monthly Recap and Insights (#023)

[Your Brand] Monthly Round-up: What We Learned in [Month]

Hello [Recipient Name],

As we wrap up [Month], we wanted to share some of the highlights:

- Feature Update: We've rolled out [feature name], which can help you [benefits of feature].
- Blog Highlight: Our top-read article: "[Title of the article]" - a deep dive into [topic summary]. [Link to article]
- Event Recap: We had a blast at [Event Name]. Missed it? Here's a quick recap and pictures. [Link to recap]
- Insight of the Month: [A key takeaway or insight you've gathered over the month, useful for your audience]

Thank you for being part of our journey. Your feedback shapes our path forward.

Warm regards, [Your Name]

V2. New Product/Feature Announcement (#024)

Introducing [Product/Feature Name]: Your New Way to [Benefit]

Hi [Recipient Name],

We've been listening and are thrilled to introduce [Product/Feature Name]!

Why you'll love it:

- Benefit One - [Short explanation]
- Benefit Two - [Short explanation]
- Special Offer: As a thank you for being with us, enjoy [offer details, e.g., "20% off for the first month"].

Dive into our latest blog post to see [Product/Feature Name] in action: [Link to the blog post]

Cheers to better experiences and more success!

Best,

[Your Name]

V3. Expert Tips and Hacks (#025)

5 Tips to [Benefit, e.g., "Boost Your Sales This Summer"]

Hello [Recipient Name],

Looking for ways to [objective, e.g., "increase your sales"]? Here are our top 5 expert recommendations:

- Tip One: [Brief description]
- Tip Two: [Brief description]

For a deeper dive into each tip and some bonus advice, check out our latest blog post: [Link]

Happy [action, e.g., "selling"]!

Best wishes,

[Your Name]

V4. Event Invitation (#026)

You're Invited: [Event Name] on [Date]

Hi [Recipient Name],

Join us for [Event Name]!

- When: [Date & Time]
- Where: [Location or "Virtual: Link to join"]

What to expect:

- [Brief description of the event]
- Exclusive insights on [Topic]
- Networking opportunities with industry leaders

Limited seats are available! RSVP by [Date]. [Link to RSVP]

Can't wait to see you there!

Cheers,

[Your Name]

V5. *Customer Spotlight and Success Story* (#027)

Spotlight: How [Customer Name] Achieved [Result]

Hey [Recipient Name],

Our community always inspires us, and today, we're highlighting [Customer Name]'s success story!

From [initial challenge] to achieving [specific result], their journey is a testament to [what makes your product/service great].

Read their full story here: [Link]

Have your own success story with us? Reply to this email! We'd love to feature you.

Stay inspired,

[Your Name]

V6. *New Blog Post Announcement Email* (#028)

New on the Blog: [Blog Post Title]

Hello [Recipient Name],

We've just published a brand new article on [Topic] that we think you'll love:

[Blog Post Title]

[Short snippet or teaser from the blog post, e.g., "Discover the 5 secrets to..."]

Why read it?

- Benefit #1 (e.g., "Unlock strategies to improve...")
- Benefit #2 (e.g., "Get insights from industry experts...")

Dive into the full article here: [Link to Blog Post]

Feedback or thoughts? Hit reply – we always love hearing from our readers!

Warmly,

[Your Name/Your Brand Name]

V7. Content Roundup Email (#029)

Top [Number, e.g., "5"] Reads from [Your Brand] This [Month/Week]

Hi [Recipient Name],

As [Month/Week] comes to a close, we've rounded up the most loved content just for you:

- [Title of First Article/Blog/Content] - [Short summary or teaser]

Read more: [Link]

- [Title of Second Article/Blog/Content] - [Short summary or teaser]

Dive in: [Link]

- ...(continue as necessary)

Whether you missed these the first time around or want to revisit a favorite, now's your chance!

To staying informed and inspired,

[Your Name/Your Brand Name]

Engagement and Retention Emails

Engagement Emails: These are designed to foster interaction between the brand and the subscriber. They often contain content that encourages the subscriber to click, read, watch, or participate in some way.

Retention Emails: These are targeted at maintaining the interest of current customers, ensuring they continue to find value in a product or service over the long term. They aim to reduce churn rates and enhance the customer's lifetime value.

Types & Examples

Engagement Emails:

- **Welcome Series:** Introduce new subscribers to the brand and set expectations.
- **Interactive Content:** Quizzes, surveys, or engaging videos.
- **User-Generated Content:** Invitations to share reviews, photos, or experiences.

Retention Emails:

- **Reactivation Campaigns:** Targeted at dormant or lapsed customers, aiming to reignite their interest.
- **Loyalty Programs:** Updates or promotions related to a loyalty program.
- **Educational Content:** How-to guides, webinars, or tutorials related to the product/service.
- **Personalized Product Recommendations:** Based on the user's purchase history or browsing behavior.

Strategies & Best Practices

Engagement:

- **Segmentation:** Tailor content based on subscriber preferences, behaviors, or demographics.
- **Dynamic Content:** Adjust content within the email based on individual user data.
- **A/B Testing:** Test different subject lines, CTAs, or content formats to optimize engagement.

Retention:

- **Regular Check-ins:** Send periodic emails asking customers about their experience or if they need assistance.
- **Special Offers:** Exclusive deals or discounts for long-term subscribers or high-value customers.
- **Feedback Solicitation:** Ask for feedback after purchases to make customers feel valued and gather insights for improvement.

Metrics to Monitor:

Engagement:

- **Open Rates:** Measure how often emails are opened.
- **Click-Through Rates (CTR):** Track the percentage of recipients who click on a link within the email.
- **Engagement Time:** How long a subscriber spends reading or interacting with the email content.

Retention:

- **Churn Rate:** The percentage of subscribers who stop using your product/service over a specific period.

- **Customer Lifetime Value (CLTV):** The net profit attributed to the entire relationship with a customer.
- **Repeat Purchase Rate:** The percentage of customers who have shopped more than once.

Engagement and retention emails are vital in nurturing and maintaining a brand's customer relationship. While engagement emails focus on capturing attention and interaction, retention emails prioritize keeping the customer involved and loyal over the long term. Both types are crucial in a holistic email marketing strategy and are integral to achieving sustained business success.

Templates

V1. Re-engagement Email: "We've Missed You!" (#030)

It's been a while, [First Name]!

Hi [First Name],

We've noticed you haven't visited [Your Brand] in a while. We've been up to a lot lately, and we think you might like some exciting new changes!

Exclusive Offer Just for You: Enjoy a 20% discount on your next purchase with code BACKAGAIN20.

Don't miss out! Come see what's new.

Warmly,

The [Your Brand] Team

V2. Feedback Request Email: "Your Opinion Matters" (#031)

Help us serve you better, [First Name]!

Hello [First Name],

Thank you for choosing [Your Brand]. Your feedback is invaluable to us. Please take a moment to share your thoughts about [specific product/service].

Bonus: Complete the survey and get a $10 voucher for your next purchase!

[Link to the feedback form]

Thank you for helping us improve.

Best,

The [Your Brand] Team

V3. Milestone Celebration Email: "Happy Anniversary with Us!" (#032)

Celebrating [X years] with you, [First Name]!

Dear [First Name],

Time flies! It's been [X years] since you joined the [Your Brand] family. Thank you for sticking with us. Here's to many more years of great experiences together!

To show our appreciation, enjoy this special [offer/gift].

Cheers to us!

Warm Regards,

The [Your Brand] Team

V4. *Tutorial & Tips Email: "Getting the Most Out of [Product/Service]"* (#033)

Pro Tips for [Product/Service] - Unlock Its Full Potential!

Hello [First Name],

Thank you for choosing [Your Brand's Product/Service]. To ensure you're getting the most out of it, we've compiled some top tips and tricks:

- **Tip One** - A brief explanation.
- **Tip Two** - Another brief explanation.

For a detailed guide, check out our tutorial here: [Link to tutorial].

Got questions? Our support team is here to help.

Best,

The [Your Brand] Team

V5. *Loyalty Reward Email: "Exclusive Perks for Our Loyal Customers"* (#034)

Because you're special to us, [First Name].

Hi [First Name],

As one of our valued customers, we're excited to introduce our new Loyalty Program! Here's what you can look forward to:

- **Early Access:** Be the first to see our new collections.
- **Exclusive Discounts:** Enjoy special deals only available to our loyal customers.
- **Birthday Surprises:** Special gifts on your special day!

Stay tuned for more exciting perks. Thank you for being a part of the [Your Brand] family.

Warmly,

The [Your Brand] Team

Event and Webinar Emails

Event and webinar emails play a critical role in an email marketing strategy, especially for businesses that host online or offline events as part of their brand engagement or educational outreach.

Purpose & Objectives

- **Awareness**: The primary objective of event and webinar emails is to inform your audience about an upcoming event or webinar.
- **Engagement**: Encouraging the recipient to interact, be it through registration, asking questions, or simply watching a teaser video.
- **Conversion**: Driving recipients to take specific actions, such as signing up for the webinar, purchasing tickets, or participating in pre-event surveys.

Types of Event & Webinar Emails

- **Announcement Emails**: These are the initial emails sent out to inform your audience of an upcoming event or webinar. They usually provide a brief overview, date, and a call-to-action (CTA) to learn more or register.
- **Reminder Emails**: As the date of the event or webinar approaches, reminder emails are sent out to ensure potential attendees have the event on their radar. This can be a series – e.g., one month before, one week before, a day before.

- **Follow-up/Thank You Emails**: Sent after the event or webinar has taken place, these emails thank attendees, provide a recap, share presentation slides or recordings, and may also solicit feedback.
- **Feedback/Survey Emails**: Post-event feedback is invaluable. It helps in understanding what went well and what areas need improvement.

Segmentation and Personalization

- **Audience Segmentation**: Not every event or webinar suits your entire mailing list. Segment your audience based on their interests, past behaviors, or demographics.
- **Personalization**: Addressing recipients by their name or referring to their past actions (like attending a previous event) can increase the email's effectiveness.

Integration with Other Platforms

- **Calendar Integrations**: Direct recipients to add the event or webinar to their digital calendars.
- **Registration Platforms**: Seamless integration with platforms like Eventbrite, Zoom, or others can streamline registration.

In conclusion, event and webinar emails are not just about informing an audience. When used effectively, they are strategic tools that can drive engagement, bolster brand loyalty, and continually offer valuable feedback to refine and improve a company's outreach efforts.

Templates

V1. Event/Webinar Announcement (#035)

Introducing Our Upcoming [Event/Webinar Name]!

Hello [First Name],

We're excited to announce our upcoming [Event/Webinar Name] on [Date] at [Time]. If you've been looking for insights on [Topic or Purpose of the Event], this is a must-attend for you!

Why attend?

- Benefit 1
- Benefit 2
- Benefit 3

Reserve Your Spot [Link to registration]

Warm regards,

[Your Name]

V2. Last Chance to Register (#036)

Last Call! Register for [Event/Webinar Name] Today!

Hi [First Name],

Time's running out! Our [Event/Webinar Name] is just around the corner on [Date]. Don't miss your chance to learn about [Topic] from the industry's best.

Register Here [Link to registration]

See you there!

[Your Name]

V3. *Event/Webinar Reminder* (#037)

[Event/Webinar Name] is Tomorrow! Are you Ready?

Hello [First Name],

Just a quick reminder about the [Event/Webinar Name] happening tomorrow at [Time]. We're all set to provide you with valuable insights on [Topic]!

Checklist for Tomorrow:

- Ensure your internet connection is stable.
- Have your questions ready.
- [Any other specific instruction].

Join the Session [Link to the webinar or event page]

Cheers,

[Your Name]

V4. *Post Event/Webinar Thank You and Feedback* (#038)

Thank You for Attending [Event/Webinar Name]!

Hi [First Name],

We're so grateful you joined us for [Event/Webinar Name]. Your participation contributed to its success!

To improve our future events, could you take a minute to provide feedback? [Link to feedback form]

In case you missed anything or want to revisit, here's the recording: [Link to the recording]

Thanks again,

[Your Name]

V5. Event/Webinar Teaser (before the full announcement) (#039)

Something Exciting is Coming Your Way!

Hey [First Name],

Get ready! We're brewing something special for all our [Brand or Community Name] members. Mark your calendar for [Date] – you won't want to miss this!

Stay tuned for more details.

Best wishes,

[Your Name]

PART II

COLD EMAIL MARKETING TEMPLATES

Business Development (BD) and Partnerships

Business Development (BD) and Partnerships are integral to a company's growth strategy. Though sometimes used interchangeably, they each have distinct characteristics and roles. Understanding them in depth, especially in cold email marketing, can help a business reach out effectively to potential partners and clients. Here's an exhaustive explanation:

Business Development:: Business Development creates long-term value for an organization from customers, markets, and relationships. It encompasses various activities, techniques, and strategies to grow and enhance a business's market position.

Role:

- **Market Analysis:** BD professionals frequently analyze market trends, identify gaps in the market, and ascertain potential growth areas.
- **Customer Outreach:** They look for new clients and customers by initiating contact, often using techniques like cold email marketing.
- **Sales Enhancement:** They're involved in refining the sales process and increasing sales volume.
- **Relationship Management:** Building and maintaining relationships with partners, stakeholders, and customers is critical.
- **Product Development:** Based on market feedback and customer requirements, BD might suggest changes to existing products or the creation of new ones.
- **Revenue Enhancement:** They employ strategies to increase revenues and profitability.
- **Strategic Planning:** BD often has a hand in shaping the company's long-term vision and strategy.

Cold Email Relevance:

- **Outreach:** Cold email campaigns can target potential clients or customers that fit a certain profile. A successful BD cold email is tailored, concise, and offers a clear value proposition.
- **Feedback Collection:** Cold emails can also gather feedback about the market, which can guide BD strategies.

Partnerships: Partnerships involve two or more organizations collaborating for mutual benefit. These could be strategic alliances, joint ventures, licensing agreements, affiliate partnerships, etc.

Role:

- **Shared Resources:** Partnerships often allow businesses to leverage each other's strengths, assets, and resources.
- **Market Expansion:** They enable companies to reach new audiences and geographies.
- **Risk and Reward Sharing:** Joint ventures and alliances often involve sharing both the risks and rewards.
- **Innovation:** Collaborative efforts can lead to new product development and innovations.
- **Cost Efficiency:** Economies of scale can be achieved when partners pool resources, leading to cost savings.
- **Branding:** Strategic partnerships can elevate a brand's image if associated with a renowned name in the industry.
- **Learning:** Partnerships foster a learning environment where companies can adopt best practices from each other.

Cold Email Relevance:

- **Initiation:** A well-crafted cold email can be the starting point for potential partnerships. It can introduce one's company, suggest potential synergies, and initiate discussions.

- **Follow-up:** Cold email campaigns can be used for following up after an initial meeting or conversation to keep the momentum going.

Overlaps & Interconnections:

Business Development often involves forming partnerships, which can lead to business development opportunities. They're intertwined in many ways:

- **Shared Goals:** Both aim for growth, market expansion, and enhanced profitability.
- **Strategic Alignment:** Partnerships can directly result from strategic planning done in business development phases.
- **Relationship Building:** Both require nurturing and maintaining strong relationships for long-term success.

In summary, while Business Development focuses on creating value through various growth strategies, Partnerships emphasize collaboration between entities for mutual benefit. Cold email marketing is a potent tool in both domains, enabling outreach, communication, and relationship building when executed correctly.

Templates

V1. Initial Introduction (#040)

Unlocking Mutual Opportunities with [Your Company]

Hi [Recipient Name],

I'm [Your Name] from [Your Company]. I've been following [Recipient's Company] and am impressed with [specific accomplishment or feature]. I believe there's an opportunity for us to collaborate and achieve even greater success together.

Would you be open to a brief chat? Let me know a time that works best for you.

Best,

[Your Name]

V2. Value Proposition Offer (#041)

Boosting [Benefit] for Both Our Companies

Hey [Recipient Name],

Our platform has helped businesses like yours achieve [specific benefit]. I'd love to explore how we can bring this value to [Recipient's Company] and simultaneously tap into your expertise for mutual growth.

Are you available for a chat next week?

Regards,

[Your Name]

V3. After an Event or Conference (#042)

Continuing our Conversation from [Event Name]

Hi [Recipient Name],

It was great meeting you at [Event Name]. Your insights on [specific topic] resonated with me, and I see potential synergies between our companies. Let's dive deeper into a potential collaboration. Does [date/time] work for you?

Cheers,

[Your Name]

V4. *Content Collaboration* (#043)

Joint Content Opportunity Ahead?

Hello [Recipient Name],

Your recent piece on [specific topic] was spot on. How about collaborating on content that bridges our expertise? I believe it could bring valuable insights to both our audiences.

Keen to hear your thoughts,

[Your Name]

V5. *Tech/Platform Integration* (#044)

Integrating our Tech for a Better User Experience

Hi [Recipient Name],

I see an opportunity for [Your Product/Service] to integrate seamlessly with [Recipient's Product/Service]. It can enhance the user experience and open new revenue channels for both of us. Are you open to discussing this?

Best,

[Your Name]

V6. *Feedback Request* (#045)

Seeking Your Expert Opinion on Our [Product/Service]

Hey [Recipient Name],

We've just launched [specific feature], and given your expertise in [relevant domain], your feedback would be invaluable. In return, I'm open to exploring how we can support [Recipient's Company].

Looking forward to your thoughts,

[Your Name]

V7. *Referral Outreach* (#046)

[Mutual Connection] Recommended I Reach Out

Hello [Recipient Name],

[Mutual Connection] mentioned you're the go-to person for [specific domain]. I believe there's potential for our companies to partner and benefit from each other's strengths.

Can we set a time to chat?

Warm Regards,

[Your Name]

V8. *Re-Engagement Email* (#047)

Reviving Our Past Conversation on Collaboration

Hi [Recipient Name],

A few months ago, we discussed a potential collaboration between our companies. I'd love to revisit that conversation and explore fresh avenues to work together.

Let's reconnect,

[Your Name]

V9. Exclusive Offer (#048)

An Exclusive Proposal for [Recipient's Company]

Hey [Recipient Name],

I have an idea that can benefit both [Your Company] and [Recipient's Company]. Before rolling it out widely, I wanted to offer it to a select few exclusively, and you're on top of that list.

Are you free to discuss this week?

Cheers,

[Your Name]

V10. Sponsorship Request Email (#049)

Unlock Mutual Benefits: Sponsorship Opportunity with [Your Event/Project]

Hi [Recipient Name],

I'm reaching out from [Your Organization/Company], and we're currently gearing up for our annual [Event/Project Name] on [Date]. Last year, we had over [Number of Attendees/Participants], and we're aiming even higher this year!

We're seeking partnerships with forward-thinking brands like [Recipient's Company] for sponsorship opportunities. By associating with our event, you'll gain:

- Extensive brand visibility before, during, and after the event.
- A chance to showcase your products/services to a targeted audience.
- Networking opportunities with industry leaders and influencers.

In return, your support will be instrumental in making the event a success. We have various sponsorship packages available, and we can customize one to match [Recipient's Company]'s goals.

Would you be open to discussing this further? I can provide a detailed sponsorship proposal for your review.

Hoping for a positive collaboration!

Best Wishes,

[Your Name]

Sales and Lead Generation

The role of sales and lead generation is pivotal in the growth and profitability of businesses, especially in the age of digital marketing. Let's break this down exhaustively.

Sales: This refers to the process of moving potential clients or leads through a funnel to convert them into paying customers. The process includes understanding the potential client's needs, presenting appropriate solutions, addressing objections, and closing the deal.

Lead Generation: This is the initiation of interest or inquiry into a company's products or services. Leads can be created for purposes such as list building, e-newsletter list acquisition, or for sales leads.

Why Are They Important?

- **Fuels Business Growth:** Businesses need a consistent inflow of new leads and customers to grow and maintain profitability.
- **Sustains Profitability:** An effective lead generation process ensures that the sales team always has new prospects to engage with, which, in turn, sustains and enhances revenue streams.

- **Competitive Advantage:** Efficient sales and lead generation processes can distinguish a company from its competitors, giving it a competitive edge in the marketplace.

Sales and lead generation are essential components of a business's growth strategy. When done right, cold email marketing can be a powerful tool in this process. However, it's crucial to approach it with a clear strategy, always putting the recipient's needs and interests first and continually refining based on feedback and metrics.

Templates

V1. B2B Introduction and Offer Email (#050)

A Partnership Opportunity with [Your Company Name]

Hi [Recipient Name],

I hope this finds you well. I'm [Your Name] from [Your Company Name], where we specialize in [specific service or product]. Having observed the way [Recipient's Company Name] operates, I see significant synergies between our companies.

Our [product/service] complements your offerings and could potentially [specific benefit, e.g., 'enhance your product line' or 'streamline your processes'].

Would you be open to discussing a potential collaboration? I'm confident that together, we can achieve mutual growth and success.

Best regards,

[Your Name]

V2. Solving a Problem (#051)

A solution for your [specific problem/challenge]

Hi [Recipient Name],

I noticed that [Their Company] might be experiencing challenges with [specific problem]. Our solution has helped companies like yours overcome this by [specific benefit].

Can we set up a call?

Regards,

[Your Name]

V3. The Mutual Connection (#052)

[Mutual Contact Name] suggested I reach out

Hi [Recipient Name],

[Mutual Contact Name] mentioned you're the go-to person at [Their Company] for [specific area]. We've helped similar businesses in [specific way].

Could we discuss how we might assist [Their Company] too?

Warmly,

[Your Name]

V4. The Compliment (#053)

Kudos on [recent achievement]

Hi [Recipient Name],

Congratulations on [recent achievement]. I believe our [product/service] could help maintain and even accelerate this momentum.

Fancy a chat?

Cheers,

[Your Name]

V5. Content Share (#054)

Thought you'd appreciate this [article/video]

Hi [Recipient Name],

I stumbled upon this [article/video] on [topic] and immediately thought of [Their Company]. It aligns with what you're doing in [specific area].

Also, our [product/service] dovetails with this nicely. Can we discuss this?

Best wishes,

[Your Name]

V6. The Stat Approach (#055)

[Impressive Stat] in [Their Industry]

Hi [Recipient Name],

Did you know [impressive stat]? Our clients have experienced this firsthand with our [product/service].

Would you like to know more?

Regards,

[Your Name]

V7. The Direct Offer (#056)

Exclusive offer for [Their Company]

Hi [Recipient Name],

We're providing select companies in [industry] an exclusive offer on our [product/service]. Given [Their Company]'s stature, we thought of you first.

Interested in the details?

Warm regards,

[Your Name]

V8. The Event Invitation (#057)

Invitation: [Event Name] for industry leaders

Hi [Recipient Name],

We're hosting [Event Name], focusing on [key topic]. It's a gathering of industry leaders; your insights would be invaluable.

Plus, our [product/service] will be showcased - it might be of interest.

Hope to see you there!

Cheers,

[Your Name]

V9. The Follow-Up (#058)

Checking in on our last chat

Hi [Recipient Name],

We discussed [product/service] a while back. Just checking in to see if now might be a better time to explore.

How's your calendar looking?

Kind regards,

[Your Name]

V10. Service Pitch to Potential Client Email (#059)

Boosting [specific metric] for [Recipient's Company Name]

Hi [Recipient Name],

I've been closely following [Recipient's Company Name] and admire how you've [specific achievement or activity]. However, I noticed a potential area where we could further elevate your [specific metric/area, e.g., 'customer engagement' or 'sales conversion'].

At [Your Company Name], we specialize in [specific service]. Our proven track record includes [a brief achievement or case study], leading to [specific results, e.g., a 25% increase in ROI].

Would you be available for a short call next week to discuss this?

Best wishes,

[Your Name]

V11. Offering a Free Trial to a Potential Customer's Email (#060)

Exclusive Trial: Experience [Product/Service] for Free

Hi [Recipient Name],

We're excited to introduce [Product/Service Name] – a game-changer in [specific industry or need]. Having seen your interest in [relevant products or services], we'd like to offer you an exclusive free trial.

- [1-2 sentences about the unique selling proposition or benefits.]

You can start your trial here [link]. We're confident you'll find it valuable and look forward to your feedback.

Cheers,

[Your Name]

Networking and Connection

Networking and connection are crucial components of cold email marketing and can significantly influence the success of a campaign.

Networking: The process of creating and nurturing professional relationships. It often involves attending events, joining groups, or leveraging platforms that facilitate interactions with other professionals in a particular industry or field.

Connection: The act of establishing a meaningful, authentic, and mutual relationship with someone. It goes beyond just knowing them; it means there's a rapport and understanding.

Foundation of Trust

- **First Impressions Matter**: A cold email is often the first interaction someone has with your brand or offer. If a mutual connection has introduced you or if the recipient knows of you through your network, there's a higher chance they'll view your email positively.
- **Building Credibility**: When recipients see that you have connections in common or recognize respected names in your network, it lends credibility to you and your message.

Increasing Deliverability and Open Rates

- **Whitelisting**: Emails from recognized connections or networks are less likely to end up in the spam folder. Being in someone's contact list or being vouched for by a mutual contact can increase your email's deliverability.
- **Recognition**: An email from a recognized name or reference is more likely to be opened and read than one from an unknown sender.

Feedback Loop

- **Improving Strategy**: By networking with peers, you can gain insights into what's working in the industry, new tools, or techniques, allowing you to refine your cold email strategy.
- **Receiving Direct Feedback**: A strong network can provide direct feedback on your approach, content, and messaging, helping you iterate and improve.

Expanding Reach

- **Referrals**: A well-networked individual can often introduce you to potential clients, partners, or influencers that you might not have reached with cold outreach alone.
- **Collaborations**: Networking can lead to partnerships where you co-create content, webinars, or events. These collaborations can expand your audience reach and provide new lists for cold email campaigns.

Overcoming Challenges

- **Bouncing Back from Mistakes**: Having a network of supporters and mentors can provide guidance and reassurance when a campaign doesn't go as planned or when facing challenges.

- **Staying Updated**: The world of email marketing is always evolving. Regulations, tools, best practices — everything changes. A solid network can help you stay updated and adapt to these changes swiftly.

Long-term Relationship Building

- **Beyond the First Email**: Networking and genuine connection mean you're not just looking for immediate results from a single email. Instead, you're building a long-term relationship, which can lead to repeat business, referrals, and collaborations.
- **Becoming a Trusted Resource**: Consistent, value-driven communication and genuine connection can position you as a trusted resource in your industry, making future cold outreach more effective.

Emotional & Psychological Benefits

- **Decreased Isolation**: Marketing can feel isolating, especially when results aren't immediate. Networking offers a support system of peers who understand the challenges and can provide encouragement.
- **Increased Confidence**: Knowing you have a robust network and genuine connections can boost your confidence when reaching out to cold prospects.

In the world of cold email marketing, where impersonal and generic messages are often ignored or discarded, networking and fostering genuine connections offer a competitive edge. They pave the way for more effective outreach, greater opportunities, and a richer, more fulfilling professional experience.

Templates

V1. Introduction and Mutual Connection (#061)

Connecting Through [Mutual Contact's Name]

Hello [Recipient's Name],

My name is [Your Name], and I was recently speaking with [Mutual Contact's Name] about [relevant topic], and they suggested I reach out to you. Given our shared interest in [Topic], I'd love to connect and discuss potential collaborations.

Best,

[Your Name]

V2. Offering Value (#062)

Thought You Might Find This Insightful!

Hi [Recipient's Name],

I've recently come across [a report/research/article] about [Topic] that I believe might be of interest to you. I'd be happy to share it with you and perhaps discuss its implications over a call.

Cheers,

[Your Name]

V3. Seeking Advice (#063)

In Need of Your Expertise on [Topic]

Hello [Recipient's Name],

I've been following your work on [specific project or topic] and am genuinely impressed. I'm currently exploring [related topic] and was hoping I could get 15 minutes of your time for some insights.

Regards,

[Your Name]

V4. Event/Conference Follow-up (#064)

Great Meeting You at [Event Name]

Hi [Recipient's Name],

It was a pleasure meeting you at [Event Name]. I found our conversation on [Topic] enlightening. Would you be open to discussing this further over coffee next week?

Best wishes,

[Your Name]

V5. *Shared Interests* (#065)

Bonding Over [Shared Interest]

Hello [Recipient's Name],

I noticed we both share a passion for [Shared Interest, e.g., sustainable energy]. I've been working on [relevant project] and thought it might be worth connecting to exchange ideas.

Warmly,

[Your Name]

V6. *Praising Recent Work* (#066)

Loved Your Recent [Article/Talk/Project]!

Hi [Recipient's Name],

Just wanted to commend you on your recent [article/talk/project] on [specific topic]. It resonated with me due to [reason]. Could we chat more about this?

Cheers,

[Your Name]

V7. Collaboration Proposal (#067)

Exploring Collaborative Opportunities

Hello [Recipient's Name],

Given our mutual expertise in [Topic], I believe we might have some interesting collaborative opportunities. I'd love to discuss a potential partnership if you're open to it.

Regards,

[Your Name]

V8. Professional Development (#068)

Seeking Guidance in [Industry/Profession]

Hi [Recipient's Name],

I'm looking to deepen my understanding of [Industry/Profession], and your career path has inspired me. Would you be open to a quick chat? Any guidance would be immensely valuable.

Sincerely,

[Your Name]

V9. Alumni Connection (#069)

Fellow [School/University] Alum Here!

Hello [Recipient's Name],

I saw that we both attended [School/University]. It's always great to connect with fellow alumni! Given our related fields, I thought it could be beneficial for us to chat.

Best,

[Your Name]

V10. New in Town (#070)

New to [City/Industry] and Seeking Connections

Hi [Recipient's Name],

I've recently moved to [City] and am trying to build connections in the [Industry]. I came across your profile and was truly impressed. Would love to grab a coffee and learn more about your journey.

Warm regards,

[Your Name]

V11. Cold Email to Potential Mentor (#071)

Seeking Mentorship in [Your Field/Area of Interest]

Hello [Recipient's Name],

My name is [Your Name], and I've been closely following your work in [specific project or topic]. Your achievements and approach have been both inspiring and guiding for someone like me who's passionate about [Your Field/Area of Interest].

I'm humbly asking if you would consider being a mentor. I understand your time is valuable, but even a brief chat occasionally would immensely benefit my growth. I'd be eager to make the most of your guidance.

Warm regards,

[Your Name]

Jobs and Opportunities

Cold email marketing, often just referred to as "cold emailing," is a method of reaching out to potential clients, partners, or customers who have had no prior relationship or interaction with the sender. The primary goal of such emails is to introduce oneself, pitch a product, service, or idea, and, ideally, initiate a conversation or transaction. When it comes to the role of "jobs and opportunities" within cold email marketing, there are several facets to consider:

Job

The term "job" in this context refers to the responsibilities and tasks of a cold email marketing strategist.

a. Research: One of the key tasks is researching potential leads to ensure the message reaches the right audience. This involves:

- Identifying target industries or niches.
- Gathering accurate contact details.
- Understanding the needs and challenges of the potential recipient.

b. Crafting the Message: The content of the email is crucial. It must be:

- Clear and concise.
- Relevant to the recipient.
- Persuasive without being pushy.

c. Personalization: The job involves tailoring messages to each recipient or segment instead of sending generic emails. This increases the chances of the email being opened and read.

d. Compliance: Ensuring that cold emails adhere to regulations such as the CAN-SPAM Act in the U.S. is vital. Non-compliance can lead to legal issues and hefty fines.

e. Testing and Optimization: Like other marketing strategies, cold emailing involves testing different approaches, analyzing results, and refining the strategy for better outcomes.

f. Building Relationships: Beyond the initial email, the job also entails nurturing relationships, following up, and eventually converting prospects into clients or partners.

Opportunities

These are the potential benefits and outcomes of successful cold email marketing.

a. Lead Generation: One of the primary opportunities is to generate new leads for the business, which can be nurtured and converted into paying customers.

b. Networking: Cold emailing can open doors to new business partnerships, collaborations, and other networking opportunities.

c. Brand Awareness: Even if a cold email doesn't lead to an immediate sale, it introduces the brand to potential clients, increasing its market visibility.

d. Feedback and Insights: Some recipients may provide feedback or insights that can be invaluable for product development, refining services, or understanding market needs.

e. Cost-Effective: Compared to other marketing strategies like paid advertising, cold emailing can be more cost-effective, especially for startups or small businesses.

f. Expansion: For businesses looking to enter new markets or target new demographics, cold emailing can be an exploratory tool to gauge interest and build initial relationships.

The role of job and opportunities in cold email marketing is a balance between the responsibilities of the strategist and the potential outcomes. A successful strategist must navigate challenges and capitalize on opportunities to drive results.

Templates

V1. Reaching Out to a Direct Contact (#072)

Mutual Interest in [Specific Industry/Topic]

Hi [Contact's Name],

I recently came across your article on [Specific Topic] and found it extremely insightful. As a [Your Profession], I share a passion for [Specific Industry/Topic]. I'd love to learn more about opportunities to work alongside your team at [Company Name]. Can we schedule a call?

Warm Regards,

[Your Name]

V2. *General Inquiry (#073)*

Exploring Opportunities at [Company Name]

Hello,

I'm highly impressed by the innovations coming out of [Company Name]. With my experience in [Your Specialization], I believe I could bring a lot to the table. Would you be open to discussing potential collaborations or positions?

Best,

[Your Name]

V3. *After a Networking Event (#074)*

Great Meeting You at [Event Name]

Hi [Contact's Name],

I enjoyed our conversation about [Topic Discussed] at [Event Name]. It made me think about how my background in [Your Experience] could align with the work at [Company Name]. Can we chat more about possible openings?

Cheers,

[Your Name]

V4. *Leveraging Alumni Connections* (#075)

Fellow [Alma Mater] Grad Exploring Opportunities

Hello [Contact's Name],

I noticed we both graduated from [Alma Mater]. As someone pursuing a career in [Your Field], I'd value any advice or insights about openings at [Company Name]. Can we connect?

Warmly,

[Your Name]

V5. *Reaching Out to a Referral* (#076)

[Mutual Contact's Name] Recommended I Reach Out

Hi [Contact's Name],

[Mutual Contact's Name] suggested I contact you regarding opportunities in [Specific Department] at [Company Name]. I believe I could be a valuable asset with my background in [Specific Skill or Experience]. Can we discuss this further?

Best,

[Your Name]

V6. *Transitioning Industries* (#077)

Transitioning from [Old Industry] to [New Industry]

Hi [Contact's Name],

Having excelled in [Old Industry], I'm excited about transferring my skills to [New Industry]. I see tremendous potential for collaboration with [Company Name]. Would you be open to a conversation?

Regards,

[Your Name]

V7. *Reapplying After a Gap* (#078)

Revisiting Opportunities at [Company Name]

Hello,

I applied to [Company Name] about [Timeframe] ago and since then have gained [Specific Experience/Skill]. I'm eager to explore how this new expertise can benefit your team. Can we talk?

Best,

[Your Name]

V8. *Cold Application for Internship* (#079)

Passionate [Field] Enthusiast Seeking Internship

Hi [Contact's Name],

I've closely followed [Company Name]'s work and am eager to learn directly from industry leaders like you. Do you have internships or training programs available? I'd love to contribute and learn.

Thanks,

[Your Name]

V9. *Exploring Freelance/Contractual Work* (#080)

Exploring Contractual Collaborations with [Company Name]

Hello,

With expertise in [Specific Service], I'm interested in exploring contractual collaborations with [Company Name]. Are there current or upcoming projects that could benefit from my skills?

Regards,

[Your Name]

V10. *Reaching Out to a Start-Up* (#081)

Excited About [Start-Up's Product/Service]

Hi [Contact's Name],

I've been following [Start-Up's Name] and am impressed by [Specific Feature/Product]. Given my experience with [Relevant Experience], I believe I can help accelerate your growth. Would you be open to a conversation?

Cheers,

[Your Name]

PART III

OTHER FORMS OF EMAILS

Educational and Training Emails

Educational and training emails play a pivotal role in the broader spectrum of email marketing. These emails are not directly promotional in nature, but they offer value to subscribers by imparting knowledge or skills. They are more than just a way to share knowledge. They are powerful tools in an email marketing strategist's toolkit, capable of fostering trust, nurturing leads, driving indirect sales, and more. The key is to ensure the content is genuinely valuable, relevant to the audience, and delivered engagingly.

Templates

V1. Welcome to the Course (#082)

Welcome to [Course Name] - Let's Get Started!

Hello [Recipient's Name],

Welcome to [Course Name]! We're thrilled to have you on board. Over the next [duration], you'll dive deep into [brief course description].

Here's what to expect:

- Module Breakdown: [Brief description of modules/topics]
- Expert Instructors: Learn from seasoned professionals in the field.
- Interactive Assignments: Engage with hands-on tasks and activities.

Getting Started:

- Log in to your account [here].
- Familiarize yourself with the course platform.
- Join our introductory webinar on [date and time].

Looking forward to an enlightening journey together!

Warm Regards,

[Your Name]

V2. *Course Reminder* (#083)

A Gentle Reminder: [Course Module Name] Starts Tomorrow!

Hey [Recipient's Name],

We hope you're as excited as we are! Just a quick reminder that [Course Module Name] starts tomorrow.

Quick Info:

- Date & Time: [specific date and time]
- Duration: Approximately [time]

Make sure to have:

- [Any specific materials or tools]
- An eager-to-learn attitude!

See you soon!

Cheers,

[Your Name]

V3. *Feedback Request* (#084)

We'd Love Your Feedback on [Course Name]

Hi [Recipient's Name],

We hope you're enjoying [Course Name]! We constantly aim to improve our courses, so we'd love to hear your thoughts.

Could you spare a minute to fill out our short feedback survey? [Link to survey]

Your insights are invaluable to us and will help shape the future of our courses.

Thanks in advance!

Best,

[Your Name]

V4. *Course Completion and Certificate* (#085)

Congratulations! You've Completed [Course Name]

Hello [Recipient's Name],

Bravo! You've successfully completed [Course Name]. Your hard work and dedication have truly paid off.

We're thrilled to present you with your course completion certificate! [Link to download certificate]

But the journey doesn't end here. Explore our other courses [link to course catalog] to continue your educational journey.

All the best,

[Your Name]

V5. Promotion for Upcoming Courses (#086)

Exclusive Peek: Our Upcoming Courses Just for You!

Dear [Recipient's Name],

As one of our esteemed learners, we thought you'd like to be the first to know about our exciting upcoming courses:

- **Course A** - Dive into [brief course description]. Starts on [date].
- **Course B** - Master the art of [brief course description]. Enrollment opens on [date].

Book your spot now and avail an early bird discount of 10%! [Link to enroll]

Happy Learning,

[Your Name]

Seasonal and Holiday Specials

Seasonal and holiday specials are a significant facet of email marketing. Leveraging these occasions can help businesses deepen their relationships with customers, drive sales, and increase brand visibility.

While seasonal and holiday specials are lucrative, they come with challenges. High email volumes during the holidays mean stiffer competition in the inbox. Also, cultural sensitivity is crucial; not everyone celebrates the same holidays. To address these:

- **Plan Early:** Prepare campaigns in advance to ensure timely and relevant delivery.
- **Segment Effectively:** Send targeted emails to improve relevance.
- **Maintain Quality:** Avoid compromising content quality in the rush of the holiday season.
- **Test and Optimize:** A/B test subject lines, content and send times to optimize results.
- **Stay Culturally Aware:** Research and respect diverse celebrations and sensitivities.

Hence, seasonal and holiday specials are pivotal in shaping an email marketing strategy. They can significantly boost sales, engagement, and brand loyalty when executed well.

Templates

V1. Thanksgiving Gratitude Special (#087)

A Special Thanks to You!

Dear [First Name],

We are counting our blessings this Thanksgiving, and you're at the top of our list!

We're offering you an exclusive 30% off our entire store to show our gratitude. Use code: **THANKS30**.

From our family to yours, Happy Thanksgiving!

Warm wishes,

[Your Company Name]

V2*. Winter Wonderland Savings* (#088)

Warm up with our Winter Deals!

Hello [First Name],

The season of giving, joy, and frosty windows is here! And to keep you warm, we've brewed up some delightful deals just for you.

Shop now and save up to **40% off** our winter collection. Use code: **WINTER40**.

Stay cozy, and happy shopping!

Cheers,

[Your Company Name]

V3*. Easter Eggstravaganza Sale* (#089)

Hop Into Our Easter Specials!

Dear [First Name],

Spring has sprung, and so have our Easter deals!

Find the perfect gift or treat yourself with **25% off** selected items. Use code: **EGG25**.

Wishing you a joyful Easter!

With love,

[Your Company Name]

V4. Summer Sizzle Sale (#090)

Dive into our Sizzling Summer Deals!

Hey [First Name],

The sun is high, and so are the discounts! Dive into our Summer collection and save big.

Enjoy **20% off** everything in store. Use code: **SUN20**.

Stay cool and shop away!

Best,

[Your Company Name]

V5. Haunted Halloween Discounts (#091)

Spooktacular Savings Inside!

Boo, [First Name]!

This Halloween, don't be haunted by missed deals. Unearth ghoulishly good savings of up to **35% off**! Use code: **SPOOK35**.

Trick or treat yourself!

Eerie regards,

[Your Company Name]

V6. 4th of July Star-Spangled Sale (#092)

Light Up Your Savings this 4th of July!

Hey [First Name],

The fireworks won't only dazzle you this 4th of July!

Celebrate freedom with **25% off** our patriotic collection. Use code: **FREEDOM25**.

Stars, stripes, and savings!

Cheers,

[Your Company Name]

V7. New Year, New Deals (#093)

Cheers to New Year Savings!

Hello [First Name],

New year, new beginnings, and... new deals! Start your year off right with a shopping spree.

Enjoy **30% off** our New Year collection. Use code: **NEWYEAR30**.

Here's to a prosperous year and fantastic finds!

Celebrate responsibly,

[Your Company Name]

Engagement Boosters

In email marketing, engagement boosters are tactics, strategies, and elements designed to increase email interaction. By leveraging these boosters, marketers aim to improve their email open and click-through rates and foster a stronger relationship with their subscribers.

Engagement boosters play a multifaceted role in email marketing, from increasing basic metrics like open and click rates to fostering long-term subscriber relationships, driving sales, and refining campaign strategies. Given the growing competition in the digital space, using these boosters effectively is essential for any email marketing strategy's success.

Templates

V1. The "We Miss You" Booster (#094)

Long time no see, [First Name]!

Hi [First Name],

We've noticed you've been a bit quiet lately. Did life get super busy? We totally get it. Just a quick note to remind you we're still here and would love to catch up!

[Maybe add an exclusive offer: Here's a 15% off just for you!]

Come back and see what's new!

Warmly,

[Your Company]

V2. *The "Exclusive Sneak Peek" Booster* (#095)

Inside Look: Something Exciting is Coming!

Hey [First Name],

We've been working on something we think you'll love. And because you're a valued subscriber, we wanted you to know first!

[Insert teaser image or link]

Stay tuned for the big reveal!

Cheers,

[Your Company]

V3. *The "Benefit Reminder" Booster* (#096)

[First Name], Are You Making The Most Of [Your Product/Service]?

Hi [First Name],

We noticed you haven't been [using a feature/checking in] lately. Did you know that with [Your Product/Service], you can:

- Benefit A
- Benefit B
- Benefit C

[Link to a guide or tutorial on how to use the product/service]

Let's maximize your experience!

All the best,

[Your Company]

V4. The "Personal Touch" Booster (#097)

Our Team's Top Picks Just For You, [First Name]!

Hi [First Name],

We thought we'd do something special today. Our team hand-picked some [products/articles/resources] that we think you'll adore:

- Pick A with a brief description
- Pick B with a brief description
- Pick C with a brief description

Enjoy exploring!

With appreciation,

[Your Company]

V5. The "Feedback Request" Booster (#098)

Your Thoughts Shape Our Future, [First Name]

Hey [First Name],

We're always aiming to better ourselves. And who better to guide us than you? It'll only take 2 minutes!

[Insert Feedback Survey Link]

As a token of our gratitude, every feedback entry gets a chance to [win a prize/get a discount].

Thank you for helping us grow!

Gratefully,

[Your Company]

V6. Polls and Surveys (#099)

We Value Your Opinion, [First Name]!

Hi [First Name],

Your feedback means the world to us! We'd love to know what you think about [topic/issue]. Please take a moment to complete our quick survey:

- [Insert Survey Link]

Your input helps us serve you better. One lucky participant will win [prize/incentive] as a token of our appreciation.

Thank you for being a part of our community!

Warm regards,

[Your Company]

V7. Refer-a-Friend Program (#100)

Friends Help Friends: Share the Love!

Hi [First Name],

Did you know you can earn rewards by spreading the word about [Your Product/Service]? It's simple:

- Refer a friend using your unique referral link: [Insert Referral Link]
- When they join or make a purchase, you both win [reward/incentive]!

Help your friends discover what you love and get rewarded for it.

Cheers,

[Your Company]

CONCLUSION

In today's fast-paced digital landscape, email marketing has proven to be an indispensable tool for businesses of all sizes. This comprehensive guide has taken you through the various facets of email marketing, from its affordability and effectiveness to the importance of personalization, segmentation, and trust development. We've explored the array of tools and terminology at your disposal, including ESPs, marketing automation, and CRM systems, enabling you to make informed decisions.

You've learned how to integrate email marketing seamlessly into your overall marketing mix, ensuring consistent branding and adherence to fundamental marketing principles. The guide has provided insights into crafting compelling email messages, including subject lines, headlines, body text, and calls to action, helping you engage your audience effectively.

We've delved into the art of cold email marketing, offering strategies to improve open rates, structure persuasive emails, and overcome common objections. With over 99 email templates at your disposal, you have a head start in creating engaging and impactful email campaigns for various purposes, from welcome emails to sales and lead generation.

Throughout this guide, we've emphasized the importance of testing, measuring performance, and adhering to best practices, ensuring that your email marketing efforts yield maximum benefits. From obtaining quick actions and feedback to increasing awareness, staying top-of-mind, and becoming a trusted sender, we've highlighted the numerous advantages that email marketing brings to your business.

As you choose email marketing tools and delve into the world of email marketing funnels, lead generation, and content creation, remember that email marketing is a dynamic and evolving field. Stay up-to-date with industry trends, adapt to changing consumer preferences, and continually refine your strategies to harness the full potential of email marketing.

With the knowledge and tools gained from this guide, you are well-equipped to embark on a successful email marketing journey that will strengthen your customer relationships, drive conversions, and ultimately contribute to the growth and success of your business. So, leverage the power of email marketing and watch your business thrive in the digital age.

Made in the USA
Columbia, SC
10 December 2024

48698077R00124